Katy Marr

THE ART OF RISING UP:

How to Stop People-Pleasing and Start Living Unapologetically

Rosebud Press

PUBLISHING COMPANY

Library of Congress Control Number: 2020908056
ISBN: 978-1-7346771-4-0
Cover design: Star. R
Interior editing: Arista. J
Cover photo ©: Katy Marr.
First Edition
9711 S Mason RD, #414 Richmond, TX, 77407
www.rosebudpress.net

For my younger brothers and sisters –
Kristen, Matthew, Kayla, Makenzie, Ryan, & Ezra. You guys are my people. My biggest hope and prayer is that you go through life courageously; resilient in the pursuit of greatness. No matter what that looks like to you. You are unstoppable

CONTENTS

INTRODUCTION

I believe that for God to take us to a new level of freedom and fulfillment in our lives, we must put ourselves in a position to be moved by God. I am naturally reserved, soft-spoken, and polite. As far back as I can remember, being reserved, soft-spoken, and polite has been mistaken for confused, shy, and meek. This created a lot of frustration for me, because while I always thought that it was my job to be polite to people, I was often mistaken for afraid and apprehensive. I have natural tendencies to be nice to people no matter the circumstance, my tendencies to comply to avoid conflict, to agree to avoid negative reactions, and for a long time, I confused silence for respect. I thought my duty in life was to stay silent and agree with people even if they treated me horribly.

I've been a people pleaser my whole life because, from a young age, something made me believe that people's approval was more meaningful than my authenticity. I started to use other people's validation as the filter through which I viewed my worth and value. That's a big issue.

The way I viewed myself was always so stagnant and inconsistent. Much like the way people's opinions are. When someone gave me praise and validated what I was doing I felt on top of the world. I felt like I had just won an award: that's how I viewed people's validation; as an award. And, as the number 3 enneagram (achiever) I am, I wanted every trophy. I wanted the feeling of being accepted and admired. But I compromised my identity and conduct to feel validated. When people had negative, pessimistic or even differing opinions, I felt worthless; like a failure, like an annoyance, like a bother, like an inconvenience I felt stupid for hours after any rejection or disapproval. The thing I've come to realize is, people's opinions are just a constant swinging pendulum of good and bad. Sometimes people have great things to say about you, and often they don't.

I decided that I was done being a slave to other people's thoughts or words towards me. I decided that if their name isn't "God" then their opinions don't matter, and their approval is not needed. We're called people-pleasers for a reason. It's a natural tendency to want to please people, but it is, in fact, impossible. So, to live your life playing small to make others happy or comfortable is unrealistic and it will rob you of your dreams. What I'm going to share is valuable information on how to break free from these chains that only drain us of our creativity, productivity, joy, and happiness.

When it comes down to it, it's about mindset, posture, and, language which are all things that must be developed. I will teach you how to develop the mindset, posture, and language it takes to overcome people-pleasing to go full force ahead in the direction of your dream life. It's time to decide what kind of posture you want to have going forward because, at the end of the day, it is a choice to either live life to meet everyone's expectations or to break down the walls of compliancy and charge in the direction of your goals with a strong, assertive, and poised posture. More than people-pleasing though, I will be sharing my story of self-limiting beliefs, overcoming past trauma, forgiving yourself and others, and learning to do the hard things to rise up into the person you were created to be. I'm writing this book to empower others to rise above mental hindrances, creative barricades, and outside voices that tell us what we can and can't be in life.

You must stop playing small, start standing up for yourself, being more direct and less compliant, overcome being a people-pleaser, stop getting walked on and taken advantage of, start telling people no, and stopover apologizing. You can be the kind of person who makes hard decisions for the betterment of your future, you can overcome societal standards, walk away from toxic habits, move on from your past trauma and pain, you can forgive and heal and be grateful for where you are. Sometimes the hardest part is just knowing *how* to do these things.

I have prayed a lot about this book before writing it and during. I have prayed so much that God would speak through me and that his perfection would meet my imperfection to create something of value for people. I want this to be a guide to help you let go and rise up from whatever has been holding you back.

This is just the set of things I've had to rise up from and I'm a firm believer that you can't teach someone something you've never done or been through. So, these chapters aren't only broken-down guides for rising up, but they are all part of my story. Things I have been through and have overcome, things God has pulled me through. I'm writing purely from my experience because I believe that we overcome battles by the words of our testimony.

I didn't want to just write a story, I wanted to write a guide inspired by my story to be a resource for people like me: people-pleasers, those with self-limiting beliefs. What all of this is, is personal development. I think it's something we all want for our lives whether we call it personal development or not. We want to live our best lives and be our best selves. We want accomplishment and success and security in our lives.

What I have learned is that we achieve that through personal development. We have to go through some training and growth to reach that best version of ourselves. I value personal development so much because it bridges the gap between who I currently am, and who I want to become. I like to think of it this way, personal development is just the act of divine improvement. When you invest in your personal development, you are working towards changing who you are, which will impact the people around you.

And when you change who you are, when you go through some character building, cut away some toxic traits and improve yourself, you will also be changing your family legacy. So it isn't some fancy word for journaling and reading more books, it is seriously life-altering when applied with intentionality and an objective to pursue the greatest version of yourself, it will drastically change your life and the lives of generations to come if you do it seriously. When you go through a process of personal refinement, getting rid of toxic behaviors, you are putting an end to what may have had a hold on your family for generations. Just the decision to set a higher standard for yourself and go through divine improvement, you are putting an end to generational curses for the betterment of not only your life but the generations after you. You are altering your family legacy when you invest in serious personal development. The way I think of it, there are two sides to personal development.

You have to think about what you want to gain, and you have to think about what you want to lose. I have broken this book down into equal parts of things to let go of and things to acquire to get to your next level of purpose and mission. There are things we have to cut out of our lives like toxic traits, bad

4

habits, unforgiveness, anger, resentment, fear, self-limiting beliefs. These are the kinds of things that can't stick with us on our way to our greatest self. These things hold us back and keep us captive to the unmotivating, mediocre, frustrating, emotional ways of our current life.

I bet we all have some traits about us we would like to get rid of. Maybe its anxiety or depression, for me, it was anger. These traits won't just go away on their own, we have to diligently work on cutting those things out of our lives. And then there are things we want to acquire, things like health, stability, a great character, a leadership mentality, better patience, more kindness, a better work ethic. The same goes for this, it takes work. Because we don't all aspire to have the same character, personal development will look different for everyone. If you struggle with people-pleasing, playing small, self-limiting beliefs, holding back, and staying quiet, this book will be a great resource for you to step out of those things and step into things like being more direct and assertive, setting boundaries and saying no, creating clear goals for yourself, developing consistency, and self-discipline. I'm huge on resources and tools. If I think something is going to help me or move in the right direction, I will throw my money at it so fast.

I just love learning how to improve my life and build my character. I love finding out how I can overcome challenges and become the best possible person I can be. I just wanted to offer something like that to others. Books have impacted me and who I am so much, I hope to bring someone the same encouragement that I've gotten from other books.

What I want to show you is how you can clean the slate and start building a foundation for the life you want for yourself and even better, the life God has for you. It's not a matter of how old you are or what your life has looked like up until this point. That is completely irrelevant to everything I will talk about in this book, so don't you worry: this content applies to everyone. If you're alive and breathing right now, this information will, one hundred percent apply to you. I want to show you how my breakthroughs have allowed me to cultivate my dreams. What you will find in this book is parts of my story as it relates to the chapter, I will share how I've overcome the difficult things and offer actual, practical steps so you can do the same. With that being said, I want to share what it means for me to rise.

PART ONE:
RISING UP

WHAT DOES IT MEAN TO RISE UP?

What does it mean to rise up? To me, it means getting on a new level, shaking off the old baggage and embracing newness. It means taking the necessary steps to improve and become a better version of myself. It means progressing every aspect of my life, physically, mentally, and spiritually. We, as humans, crave progress. We crave the feeling of newness and improvement in our lives. Even if you're someone who despises change, I'm sure there's a part of you that desires more for your life. It's an instinct for humans to continuously move forward and cultivate more; to want better for themselves.

It's natural to achieve something more fun, more fulfilling, happier, and more adventurous. Take, for example, any time you have had a goal. As soon as you reach one of these goals, it's not long before you're on to the next big adventure. Our never-ending goals and future aspirations are proof that we constantly have a dream in our hearts. We always have a desire to move forward in the direction of our dreams and achieve higher levels of success. We are constantly in forward motion.

No matter what success looks like to you, we all have the same approach to it; to rise up. When it comes to our goals, we are all headed in the same direction; forward. Anything worth having takes work, that's an obvious fact. To achieve anything, we need to *rise* to the occasion and do the work necessary. But that's not all, I've learned that one of the most important things when it comes to rising to a new level is that to get to a new level, you have to cut off the chains that have been holding you in this one. You can't bring this insecurity, doubt, shyness, timid behavior with you to this next level.

It's human nature to crave progress, to continue adapting, changing, and refining ourselves, and our lives. I'd be worried if you didn't want more for your life. We have all heard it said before, your new life will cost you your old one. I believe that where God wants to take you in this next chapter of your life is so brilliantly more than you could ever imagine. But before that can come to fruition, you need to let go of some things weighing you down. You simply can't rise to the next level in your life while holding all the weight you've been carrying around.

It's time to cut the fat of your life and let go of your past, tainted relationships, guilt and shame, self-limiting beliefs, wishy-washy decision making, or old toxic behaviors. If you want newness in your life, it will take newness in every aspect. It will require you to develop certain habits. One of my favorite stories in the *Bible* is when the Israelites had fled Egypt. The Israelites lived in bondage to the Egyptians where they were slaves. God rescued them and brought them out of Egypt and to me, this could have, alone, been an awesome story.

These people were trapped under a ruler who kept them as slaves, but God sends Moses to rescue them. God does the impossible and leads them out of slavery. And everyone lives happily ever after. But that wasn't the end. God had envisioned for them the Promise Land; a new level, a new place to start fresh.

But the Israelites didn't bounce from level to level to level. They spent forty years in the wilderness. God needed to shape these people who had been living as slaves and turn them into strong warriors who could fight and fend for themselves. They needed to be refined and strengthened before they even stepped foot in the promised land. And this process takes time. If you think about this story, it can be applied to our lives.

We don't bounce from level to level effortlessly. Maybe you've recently been rescued from your Egypt, maybe you've come out of a season of pain or scarcity or struggle. If that's the case, I'm so glad you're here because the next step is laying a foundation for an immensely better future for yourself.

Bigger dreams mean bigger and harder work. It means developing into a stronger and smarter person. It means healing and letting go of past mistakes and hardships. If we can't accept the fact that we must invest in healing and letting things go, we won't make it to the next level. I want *The Art of Rising Up* to be a guideline for foundation building. Strong foundations lead to strong structures. If you want to rise up, the first part is chipping away at the old. The second part is laying a solid foundation.

That's why I broke this book up into two parts with this same concept in mind. The main purpose of writing this is to lead people to grow and to inspire people to rise above adversities in pursuit of their purpose. Fun fact, *this* is my first book. I've never written more than a five page essay for English class. I find myself nervous and anxious as I write this. I know it won't be perfect, but my prayer is that it corresponds with the right people. Books have impacted my learning and developed my mindset so much; I want to add to that in hopes that my story and what I've learned in my twenty years of life might inspire someone else. I believe that there is power in sharing our stories with people and sharing how we've overcome our battles.

I guarantee people are reading this who can relate to my story. I know the frustration that comes along with being in a rut. Feeling uninspired and stuck. I know what it feels like to wish for a spark to flame within you and inspire you to dive into something exhilarating. If my story inspires one single person to get up, shake off the dust, raise their ambition, take their dreams seriously, set some goals, conquer some internal battles, forgive people who hurt them, let go of trauma, heal, and rise up to, then it is well worth it.

KNOWING OUR IDENTITY IN JESUS

From about the time I was seven-twenty years old, I saw myself however people made me feel. If someone made me feel stupid, I saw myself as stupid. If someone made me feel annoying, I adopted the identity of annoying- if someone got mad at me, I saw myself as someone who made people mad- if someone made me feel inferior to them, then that's exactly how I saw myself too. I, myself have often struggled with my identity and I have also seen others battle with their identity. It's a tough thing to get a grasp on because in a world that tells us we're not good enough, not worthy enough and not valuable enough, we're supposed to believe that we are.

We seem to place our worth in what the world says about us whether it's direct or indirect criticism. Our society is so virtually connected and so many random standards have been placed on us. The internet has decided what success looks like, what healthy looks like, what beautiful looks like, what greatness looks like. We indulge in the popular, yet unrealistic standards deemed by random people on the internet and that is what we strive for. I believe that the root of people-pleasing and playing small is in an identity issue. At least that was the case for me.

When there is a disconnect in our identity and who we are, it leaves so much room for false representations of who we're supposed to be. I believe that when we struggle with pleasing people, seeking their constant approval and validation, and worrying about their thoughts and opinions towards us it's because we struggle to be grounded in who we are. My issue was that I didn't know who I was, so I was looking at everyone else to tell me who I was. I was looking at anyone and everyone to tell me if I was right or wrong. I asked for the approval of my ideas, my goals, my plans, my looks, my thoughts, my views, my beliefs. I invited people to tell me if I was right or wrong, good or bad because I didn't know for myself. My identity wasn't grounded in anything. So not only would I invite unnecessary feedback on my life, I ended up getting a lot of unsolicited feedback on almost everything because I became the kind of person who would open myself up to receiving the random judgment of other people. I became the kind of person who only felt right about what I was doing if people around me thought it was good. On top of that, if someone *did* disapprove of my choices, I felt the need to explain myself and further seek validation. The problem with not being grounded in your identity is that you look to other people to tell you who you are. That's never how it was supposed to be. Other people aren't supposed to have the right to validate you because we've already been validated by God. Before we can get into anything we have to establish this belief.

I believe that we struggle with things like people-pleasing, playing small, other people's opinions, self-limiting beliefs, and seeking validation and approval from outside sources because we fail to remember that our identity is in Christ first and foremost. What He says about us trumps all other feedback. We are created in the image of our perfect God (*New International Version*-Genesis 1: 27). We are God's temple and His Spirit dwells within us. We get way too distracted worrying about how the world views us; perfect Instagram pictures, counting the number of likes, sitting at work wondering if your colleagues "like" you when the creator of the universe calls you loved, worthy, purposed, treasured, justified, redeemed, free, accepted, and blameless. Most importantly, he calls us His.

We belong to a God who has a detailed plan for our lives. This, right here, should be enough for us to let go of impressing others or seeking validation. We have been predestined by God for greatness for His glory- talk about some great news. I don't have to worry about impressing anyone, getting approval or a psychological permission slip signed by anyone because of what God has already said about me. By nature, I like recognition, after all, I am a number three, (the achiever) on the Enneagram, and my love language is words of affirmation. So I like to reach goals, make things happen, achieve big things, and do more than the people around me, AND I like to be recognized for my hard work/accomplishments. Maybe that makes me super self-absorbed in some eyes, but I just love when people reassure me. I love when people say good things about me- I love when people appreciate and recognize me. That's how I most feel loved. But even with this personality, although it's not a bad personality, I must always remind myself to not put so much value on what other people think about me and remember what God *says* about me.

When you find your identity in Christ, you are free from having to only feel good when people around you tell you that you're good. Because as long as we are looking everywhere else for a pat on the back when we do something, we will live like prisoners to outside validation. You have to get extremely good at seeing yourself the way God sees you and you won't feel trapped or weighed down by the need to get approval from anyone else nearly as much. When I am fully in tune with how God thinks of me, I feel so much more empowered to follow through with the vision He's given me. I don't have to rely on my understanding or limited skillset.

He does not call the qualified, He qualifies the called. He gives us a vision and equips us along the way. I don't have to worry about being perfect because God says I can do all things through the strength He provides me. So how do we get good at viewing ourselves the way God does? Make it a habit to accept who Jesus *says* you are. Make a conscious decision to start perceiving that as truth instead of the lies you tell yourself or the fickle opinions of others. I will dive deeper into opinions and self-limiting beliefs but we can't get over those things until we get a strong grounding in our identity.

We were made to have an identity in Christ; to be like him. We were made to take after the likeness of Jesus, not the world. When we feel pressured to do things the way everyone does them, to act the way young adults act, to do life the way society perceives the best way, when we follow cookie-cutter societal standards for life, we are ultimately trading in God's perfect plan for a flawed, insufficient, unsustainable version of what was intended to be purposeful, abundant, and incredible. When we don't have our identity firmly placed in

God, we fall for everything society deems good and successful.

That is a huge problem because true satisfaction and abundance are found in Jesus when He's not our source of fullness, richness, and joy, we get fake, watered down versions of the best that God has originally planned for us. I hope you have the audacity and the faith to put your belief in Jesus and stop looking to the world to fill the void in your heart. You'll be searching your whole life to find what God is giving you with open arms and all you have to do is say yes. Worldly satisfaction is temporary and when it runs out you have to go run and find another source. With God, that's forever. His love never runs out. Nothing we could ever do will change the way he views us. That's just not something this world has to offer us. Ephesians 2:9 tells us "For it is by grace you have been saved, through faith. And this is not your own doing; it is the gift of God, not a result of works, so that no one may boast." (*New International Version*) With God, we aren't strangers and we have a place in God's house. We always have a seat at the table. As someone who has always struggled with fitting in and thinking I have to be cool enough to sit with certain people, I know that with God, there is always a place for me and I don't need to squeeze my way in or continuously prove to people that I deserve to be there. He welcomes us and there is always a place for us; we don't have to compete for God's love or attention. In addition to that, I believe that God has a plan for a place you are meant to be.

I don't know if you can relate to this or not, but a lot of times in my life, I felt like I had to always squeeze my way into friend groups or social groups otherwise, I was left out. More often than not, I have felt like there wasn't a place for me where I was trying to be involved.

What the Holy Spirit put on my heart is that that's not how I was supposed to go through life; squeezing my way in, fighting for a place or a spot, or *proving* that I deserved to be there. At least not in atmospheres such as friend groups or community. What I learned is that God desires for me to be somewhere where I am welcome and loved and somewhere I have a place and I don't have to go through my life feeling like I'm left out or not included unless I fight for it. I share because I believe that the same applies to you. God has a place for you where you can *belong* and not just a place you can participate in or stand on the sidelines. "So, you are no longer a slave, but God's child; and since you are his child, God has made you also an heir." (*New International Version*-Galatians 4:7) You are a child of a King. When you say yes to a life with Jesus and accept Him as your LORD and savior, that's it. You're no longer a slave but a child of God and that makes you royalty. Imagine how much different we would live if we knew every day the profound significance of our identity being in Christ. I bet we would go through life excited. I bet we would stop feeling inferior to other people. I bet we would look at people, not as our competition, but as our equal- I bet it would change the way we talk to ourselves- I bet we would see ourselves as valued and purpose-filled.

And I'm sure we would stop looking at the world and media to tell us who were supposed to be and we would look to God for our purpose. Developing a strong grounding in God's vision for your life is powerful. Living your life with a strong grasp of your identity in Christ is worth getting good at it. And I'm sure we would stop looking at the world and media to tell us who were supposed to be and we would look to God for our purpose. Developing a strong grounding in God's vision for your life is powerful. Living your life with a strong grasp of your identity in Christ is worth getting good at it. I want you to get good at it because when you do, you will always have your worth grounded in that. God is unmoving, unwavering, consistent, and firm in the way He thinks about you. His thoughts about you don't switch off randomly. He isn't for you one day and against you the next. What He says about you remains true throughout all trails in life-so, while we're over here tearing ourselves apart because of the disapproval and harsh feedback from our fellow humans, the creator of the universe is admiring you for everything.

What was always so crazy to me is that I am known better by God than anybody else, yet deeper loved by Him than anyone else. God knows every little thing about me. He knows how many hairs are on my head, He knows my thoughts and feelings that nobody else does; He knows my deepest fears and darkest secrets and it's not all pretty, I'm sure we can all relate to that. The point is, God knows you better than anyone, yet He loves you more than anyone ever could.

A relationship and identity within God means being deeply known and deeply loved at the same time. I wonder how many people would love me if they knew all my flaws and imperfections, the mistakes I make, and the ugly things I've walked through; maybe some, but not many. But God knows all of that and more and He still loves me. So why would I ever base my worth off any other love? When people disapprove of you, they are just disapproving of something they don't fully know. God knows all of you and loves you more than you could even imagine, so don't waste any more time worrying about if people love you or not. So, as we get into the nitty-gritty, it's so important to understand who you are. You must establish a grounded identity because otherwise, your view of yourself is just as much up in the air as everyone's fickle opinions. How you view yourself shouldn't be up in the air, available to anyone to tamper with. When we don't know our identity, that's what's happening, we are allowing people to tamper with our self-image- that can be a very depleting thing. I struggle with this in groups of people. When I'm around other people more than I'm around God, I can sense feelings of inferiority, insecurity, and comparison. As people-pleasers, we have to constantly remind ourselves of who we are and *who's* we are.

It almost has to be a daily ritual because our natural tendency is to look to others for approval and if we go too long without having grounded identity and knowing our worth and value in the Lord, we will let others do the dictating. Other people don't have the right to claim you worthy or unworthy so stop letting them. There is also a huge disconnect between who we *are* and who we *want* to be which can lead us to confusion about our identity. For example, I have a very clear vision for who I want to become. I think about it all the time. But when it came to who I am right now, my mind drew a blank. What do you do when you know who you want to become but have no idea who you are now? You have to start seeing yourself as the future best version of you.

That person won't just appear one day when you have more money or a better house. You have to embody that person and become that person every day whether your circumstances are peachy or not. Speak, walk, act, dress, serve, lead, like your future best self and watch yourself turn into that person. How we view ourselves has a powerful hold on what our reality looks like. If anything has ever shaken me back into knowing my identity in Jesus, it was being told that God created me, therefore, I was born with value. God created you – He formed you in the womb, He customized you. You were fearfully and wonderfully made and God does not make mistakes. Stop letting people tell you your value when it was never up to them. Nothing is qualified to determine your worth.

God knew you from the very beginning and he called you valued, treasured, and worthy. All other opinions are unqualified. I hope that this chapter has inspired you to view yourself with the lenses through which God sees you. I didn't encapsulate the depth of how precious our identity in Jesus is. My few pages on identity didn't do justice on the wild love God has for us. But I hope that it has lit a spark in your heart, and you can go into the rest of this book knowing and feeling a little more clarity about just how important how you view yourself is.

It makes the rest of it make sense. If my identity is in Jesus, if He created me and brought me life, if he knows all my flaws, all my mistakes, yet he calls me purposed and loved, if he calls me His child, His beloved, then it makes it so much simpler to go through the process of rising up from a worldly point of view. I hope that you can rise up from a worldly point of view with your eyes on God and your heart on His purpose.

PEOPLE-PLEASING

My people-pleasing habit developed out of fear of people getting mad at me. The earliest memory I have of someone, other than my parents, getting mad at me was my fourth-grade teacher. My mom homeschooled me from kindergarten through third-grade, which was amazing. But fourth grade rolled around and my parents decided to send my sister and me to a small public school in the mountains where we lived. I was excited. I didn't know what to expect because all I knew was my home and Mom and what our day-to-day looked like as she gave me my education.

I was in girl scouts at that time, so I knew I liked hanging out with my friends and having a social outlet so, in my mind, the school was going to be awesome and such fun. I was excited about gym class and having my desk and packing my lunch every day; I was excited to have more friends and feel involved in a class. I remember my mom and dad walking my sister and me to our classes. It was everything I expected: gym class was a blast, I loved my desk and getting to organize it, I was happy to be a part of a class and away from home for a little.

What I didn't expect was the way I would have been treated by the people around me. Looking back, I wouldn't say I was bullied, fourth grade kids aren't always peachy, that's just reality. I mean I did get left out and, at times, kids made it obvious that they didn't want to be around me. Being an eight-year-old little girl, that broke my heart. That sort of thing never really changed. I struggled with that through middle school and high school as well. The girls had their girls and I was rarely one of them.

They kept me around just in case they didn't have anyone else to talk to or hang out with but most of the time, I was left out and felt invisible. Kids weren't the best to me. Lots of kids aren't the best people in the world to be around. But what shook me up as a new student, a brand-new public-school student, was how awfully my teacher treated me. She would use sarcasm to belittle me in front of the entire classroom. If I went up to the board to try and solve a math problem, she would dismiss me at the first sign of struggle.

When she did sit down with me one-on-one to teach me, I was struggling with a math concept. She was short with me and when I gave the wrong answer, she threw her head down on the desk and dismissed me- I was in tears- I felt hopeless and confused and hurt. Mind you, I'm a little kid and a grown woman is getting mad at me because I couldn't figure out a math problem. I hated the feeling of my teacher being mad at me, it made me feel so insecure and inferior and stupid and worthless. At that moment, my teacher constantly getting mad at me translated to:

1. WHEN I TRY NEW THINGS, I WILL BE MET WITH JUDGMENT

2. MY AMBITIONS WILL ANNOY PEOPLE

3. IF I MAKE A MISTAKE, PEOPLE WILL GET MAD AT ME

4. I SHOULDN'T PUT MYSELF OUT THERE

5. I SHOULDN'T TRY NEW THINGS

From that moment on, I had such a distinct feeling of shame and regret for putting myself out there. It left such a bad taste in my mouth. That was followed by another series of trying new things just to be met with harsh reactions. I know that we have all had our fair share of bad bosses, poor leaders, and harsh teachers. I had a series of trying new things with poor leaders and people who did not know how to teach. I found myself in many situations where people were disappointed with me for not following through on an expectation never discussed.

It made me sensitive to other people's emotions towards me, I felt flooded with guilt anytime I made someone upset; I felt like a failure when I disappointed people. I felt the weight of my emotions so heavily when something I did made someone else react negatively that it caused me to drawback. I wanted to avoid those feelings at all costs. I just wanted people to be happy with me, so I walked on eggshells around them, kept quiet, kept my head down and never tried new things if it meant avoiding conflict or negative reactions. I became obsessed with not getting in trouble. I knew how much easier it was to just be reserved and act like a good girl; to be polite, to keep to myself, to close my mouth.

I learned that being quiet and non-assertive made situations more peaceful. I didn't want anyone to be mad at me. I didn't want to get in trouble or get any backlash for having differing thoughts or views and this is just one of a couple of different forms of people-pleasing that I'll dive into in this chapter. I wanted to share where it started for me. I believe that people-pleasing is rooted in fear and it causes us to play small and limit ourselves and our creativity. The four fears that people-pleasing develops from are:

- FEAR OF ANGER
- FEAR OF MAKING OTHERS FEEL BAD
- FEAR OF JUDGMENT AND CRITICISM
– FEAR OF CONFRONTATION

Now that we understand that people-pleasing *is* rooted in fear, we know the core of what needs to be changed here. I explained briefly how my fear of people being angry with me to lead to people-pleasing. You probably have your own story. Nobody likes it when people are mad at them. But it became a fear of mine and it became almost imperative that I don't step on anyone's toes and make them mad. What I have learned is that we don't need to tiptoe around people so they don't get angry.

If who you are as a person and normal mistakes, we all make is enough to make someone *angry*, they've got bigger issues than you. We should all have enough self-control over our emotions that we don't get angry at people for mistakes or annoyances. As far as the fear of making others feel bad, it's just another tricky task we put on ourselves. This only causes us to act unauthentic because we tone down everything to not hurt anyone's feelings. There's nothing wrong with not wanting to make others feel bad, but it shouldn't come at the cost of your authenticity. In many situations, I felt the need to lower my voice, not have as much fun and not go full out with whatever I'm doing because I didn't want to make anyone else feel bad.

It's not that I thought that I'm so much better than everyone around me, but because I knew how it felt to be the girl who felt inferior and not good enough. But those were my insecurities, nobody should have to tone down their happiness and passion to cater to those insecurities. I did not and do not need to do that for others and *neither* do you. If you want to make others feel adequate, important and talented, point it out. Tell them about their great qualities. Hiding your zest for life, excitement and passion won't make anyone feel better about themselves. You're not protecting anyone by hiding yourself.

When it comes to our fear of judgment and criticism, we as people pleasers need to get over our fear of other people's thoughts and reactions toward us. God never said that our purpose here on earth was to satisfy other humans with our every move. That is not only impossible, but it keeps us from pursuing our true purpose and calling in life. When you have a mission or a goal or a dream, but you try to make everyone else happy along the way, you forfeit the full completion of your dream. People-pleasing only waters down our goals because you really can't please everybody. So why strive for that? Why feel obligated to that? And our fear of confrontation? It's not something to be afraid of.

People's backlash and negative reactions might be nerve-wracking, but if there is something or someone that needs to be confronted, you should be able to do that without psyching yourself out because you don't want anyone to get upset, judge you, or feel bad. If you haven't noticed the pattern by now, here it is: we don't want to make anyone upset. We want people to like us, or at least be happy with us. We hate feeling like we made someone irritated, angry, or annoyed.

We also don't want people to think judgmental thoughts about us. We don't want to hurt any feelings, make anyone feel bad, or ruffle any feathers. So, we tiptoe around people to avoid those reactions, hence, people-pleasing. We live life apologetically but still get mistreated and misunderstood. We often don't confront anyone who has treated us poorly because we don't want to make anyone upset. Here is a visual made by yours truly:

We don't want to make anyone upset, hurt anyone's feelings, ruffle feathers or get judged.

So we tip-toe around people to avoid those reactions (people-pleasing)

We play small, we don't establish boundaries & we live apologetically.

When we are mistreated, we don't confront anyone or stand up for ourselves because. . .

And that's the crazy cycle that goes over and over and over in the life of a people-pleaser. It's important to be aware of that cycle so you know what we are trying to break here. But it is also important to know that you are a recovering people-pleaser and you don't owe it to anyone to live your life like that. The way I see it, you can either chase after your dreams or you can chase after the approval of others. But you can't chase two rabbits at once. You must choose one and people-pleasing is never a worthy goal. It's not attainable, it's fickle, people's emotions fluctuate by the minute.

I know it feels good when people are happy with you. And I know how incredibly discouraging it feels when you're judged, criticized, disapproved, dismissed, contradicted, shut down, suppressed, looked down on, or shamed for your ambition or your vision. It's not fun. It hurts. Especially when that comes from people you love; your family or closest friends. I think that a mistake we make as a society is, we put too much expectation on the reactions of people around us. What I mean by that is, we have great, spectacular, exciting dreams and we make the mistake of expecting everyone to love it as much as we do.

First of all, nobody will love your dreams as much as you do. Not even your mom. And that's because they're *your* dreams. Even more so, nobody will be nearly as ecstatic about your ideas as you are, and a lot of people will disapprove. Whether it's out of love or judgment, it will 100% happen to you. So, we have two facts.

1. **YOU WILL NEVER MAKE EVERYONE AROUND YOU HAPPY AND PLEASED**
2. **YOU WILL ALWAYS BE DISAPPROVED BY SOMEONE NO MATTER WHAT**

I don't use the words "never" and "always" lightly. Those are strong words and most of the time, in the context in which we use those words . . . they end up not being true. But this is one of the rare times I've found "never" and "always" to be completely factual. I think we should take that as a sign and stop striving for such absurdly unrealistic things. Think about it. Jesus is King and not even He gets everyone.

Not even the creator of the universe gets everyone's approval. You can't win them all so you might as well focus on doing the best you can with what you have and smash the goals you set out to achieve. My fear of people getting mad at me caused me to do things just to be nice to people. I would say yes to avoid conflict. I would agree to things because I felt obligated to. I would make decisions just so people would like me.

I would say "sorry" for things that weren't my fault and I wouldn't stand up for myself when someone treated me badly. I cared more about people liking me (or at least not being mad at me) more than I cared about being my most authentic self. I won't sit here and tell you all to "just be yourself " because if that was the solution, we wouldn't be having this issue right now. But what if I told you that maybe other people's emotions towards you has a lot more to do with them than they do with you? We cannot control other people's emotions, no matter how amazing we are. I believe that when we stop directing our efforts to satisfy the emotions of other people and start being secure within ourselves and our own decisions, that's when we start to see change.

People act however they want to and say whatever's on their mind. If someone disapproves of you or your decision, odds are you will hear about it. If you decide to allow that to rule your behavior and dictate your own emotions, that's on you. As I said, people's criticism can either come from a place of love or a place of judgment. You can certainly receive constructive criticism with open arms, and you definitely should because not all criticisms are bad, you get to *decide* who you listen to. Understand the difference between embracing intentional advice from someone who wants the best for you and accepting all the murmuring and making efforts to please.

What I can tell you is that walking on eggshells around people to avoid conflict or ruffled feathers doesn't do anyone any favors. It might keep you in your comfort zone or "safe" zone, but I promise you that nothing great is ever accomplished in those premises. Stop being afraid of people being mad at you. Stand your ground and do what you know is right and what aligns with your mission. People will act however they want to, don't allow that to be your decision-maker. I'm not saying you have to go around and completely disregard how your actions might impact other people. I'm saying don't tip-toe around people.

Don't live as a watered-down version of your best self so that other people feel more comfortable. Don't make decisions based on if you think it will make someone mad. Some of the most impactful, influential people have ruffled a lot of feathers and made a lot of people uncomfortable. When you're after greatness, that's just part of it, not everyone will feel peachy about what you're doing, how you live your life, what you do for a living, etc.. If everyone around you seems pleased, you should be worried.

I take disapproval as a sign to keep going. The approval and validation of the people around you is not a secure platform to base your decisions off of. The most important thing here that I want you to understand is that *people-pleasing is not what God wants for you*. I gained so much freedom when I truly understood that we aren't here to please anyone. We are here to please God and co-create with the maker of the world.

He wants us to work alongside him in cultivating, building, creating, innovating, and pursuing our mission in life. It was never about pleasing humans and here is how I know:

"For am I now seeking the approval of man or God? Or am I trying to please man? If I were still trying to please man,

I would not be a servant of Christ." (*New International Version*-Galatians 1:10)

"Whatever you do, work heartily, as for the Lord and not for men"
(*New International Version*-Colossians 3:23)

Beware of practicing your righteousness before other people in order to be seen by them." (*New International Version*-Matthew 6:1)

"Do not be conformed to this world, but be transformed by the renewal of your mind, that by testing you may discern what is the will of God, what is good and acceptable and perfect." (*New International Version*-Romans 12:2)

"What then shall we say to these things? If God is for us, who can be against us?" (*New International Version*-Romans 8:31)

"Owe no one anything, except to love each other, for the one who loves another has fulfilled the law." (*New International Version*-Romans13:8)

God makes it clear that our job is to love people, not to seek the approval of people. We have God's approval by faith. I don't know about you, but I think that this is such great news. It's so freeing to know that the only opinion that matters has already deemed me worthy. I don't need to cater to the emotions or opinions of other people. Mamie L. Pack said this: "When you live a life in bondage to people-pleasing, you are constantly swayed by the fickle opinions of people instead of living free in the steadiness of our unchanging God.'' Who else thinks it would be so much better to live free in the steadiness of our unchanging God? I would rather have that than the applause and validation of a million people.

What people have to offer us is a temporary rush of pats on the back. It feels good to have recognition, but it is temporary. What God has to offer is constant, never changing approval and love. More than that though, it also comes with lasting peace and freedom. We need to stop striving to please other people and gain their validation. Why? Because it is not what God wanted for us. People's validation is limited and fleeting- it will change repeatedly. When we live to please people, we will always feel lacking- we will always feel not good enough, insufficient.

It will lead us to only make decisions just to gain approval instead of doing the things God has placed on our hearts that will drive us to our goals. Because we should not live in fear of rejection or dismissal. We should not feel constrained to other people's reactions to us. It is not our job to go through life making sure everyone is happy and pleased. It is not our obligation to walk on eggshells around people and play small so they can feel more comfortable. Because there is nothing humble about hiding the real you.

HOW:

Practice the way you conduct yourself. If you are naturally reserved, practice sharing your real thoughts and feelings with boldness. If you are naturally shy or soft-spoken, practice small acts of outspokenness: say good morning to each of your coworkers in the office tomorrow. If you naturally feel the need to draw back so other people don't feel uncomfortable, practice being more open and confident. It is all about practicing your conduct and becoming the kind of person who is extremely secure and confident in sharing their true thoughts and ideas. It can be done through small acts of boldness each day. Some people will notice a change.

They will notice your boldness and stepping out of the people pleasing ways. Some people won't notice or won't think much of it and continue to treat you the same way. But you're not doing it so people can view you differently. You're doing it so that you can feel secure and grounded in your character and not feel the need to cater to everyone else's likes and dislikes about you. You aren't here on this earth just to be who everyone else wants you to be or thinks you should be. A lot of the time, people only validate you or show approval and excitement if you are doing, saying, being, believing what they do, say, are, and believe.

If it matches, they will high five it. If it doesn't match, you'll be judged and called out. The thing is, we all have differing views. But too many people have been programmed to believe that their beliefs are the best and truest and that all other views are garbage. And that doesn't make you want to share your authentic self around those people. Believe me, I get it. I understand going for it just to be shot down and ridiculed because your thoughts and ambitions don't match someone else's.

Some people will tear you down for having a different opinion about the smallest things. People love to make their opinions and beliefs superior. And no, it does not make us want to share our real thoughts with people, it makes us want to hide and fake it out, so we don't risk getting bashed for who we are. But the more we practice executing boldness concerning who we are, we can more live a life of authenticity instead of a life of constant discomfort and hiding just to make other people feel more comfortable. You deserve to live a life of boldness and excitement. You deserve to be yourself, enthusiastic, excited to share your true views, and not afraid of who doesn't like them or give them any attention.

Attention is not what life is about. I know that we have been conditioned to think that it is, but that is the biggest lie of our generation. It's not about attention. It's not about how many likes or followers you get. It's not about how many congratulations you get, how big the applause is, or whether people think your ambitions are cool or not. It's not about that at all. It's about the value in your vision and what it is going to do to impact your life and the lives of the people around you. If you're doing something just to get attention, you might win at that game, but it is fleeting.

Attention is fleeting and temporary, but the impact is long-lasting and enduring. Anyone can redirect their attention to the next best thing. But the impact has a lasting effect that doesn't leave nearly as quick. So instead of striving for attention or people to be pleased with you, strive to leave an impact on people's lives. Strive to make a difference with your ambitions, to do something of value with your talents, to be extremely generous and kind. If all you're doing is trying to turn heads and get people to notice you, you will have to forfeit your authenticity for cheap things that get attention. Anything worth pursuing takes a lot of time and patience.

For a long time, people won't notice. They won't see the vision, they won't care what you're working on, they won't show any interest at all. Allow yourself permission to have your vision and aspirations be unseen for a while. Manifest in private, work in private, build in private. Because the goal isn't to be noticed or seen or applauded for your efforts, it's to make an impact and create something of significance so that when the time comes, the right people will see it and correspond with it. I understand wanting recognition, that's like my love language.

It's okay to want that, but make sure that the core of your why is deeper than a few fleeting moments of recognition that will soon pass. Not everyone needs to know what you're up to. Being seen and validated for your work does not make the work significant. The impact it has on people is what makes it significant. There is value in keeping your dreams between you and God for a season because it teaches your heart that even without anyone's high fives or great job affirmations, you can still pursue and create something extremely significant. It teaches us that God is all we need and through Him, we can do all things.

The *Bible* doesn't say I can do all things through the approval of humankind and worldly attention. It says, in Philippians 4:13 that, "I can do all things through Christ who strengthens me." (*New International Version*-Philippians 4:13) Other people's attention is completely irrelevant and therefore their approval and attention are not needed. When we can approach our ambitions with this mindset, it will be a major game-changer in your life. Not only will it allow you to rely on God more than other people's attention, but it will allow you to go through life not feeling a need for people to tell you if what you're doing is okay or not.

You won't need people to tell you if your idea is good. You won't need anyone else's excitement for you or enthusiasm, you'll be excited all on your own and even if nobody ever knows what you're up to, God is working on something big in your life and it's just a matter of time before it is built into something that will significantly impact the right people for the right reasons. Your mission should not be to get noticed, it should be to come alongside God and let His validation *move* you in the right direction. Rest in the fact that God has already validated you and you don't need to go hunting for it every 5 minutes. That should give you a lot of peace.

I do, however, understand the value of sharing our goals.

When we proclaim or goals, it sets a kind of accountability. When you tell people what you are working for, you feel a greater pull to actually follow through rather than to keep it inside forever and never share with anyone because you know people are watching you. Verbalizing your goals is a powerful thing when done with the right intentionality. My point is that we shouldn't be sharing what we're working on in hopes of getting immediate recognition or attention, most of the time people won't understand or support right away. And it shouldn't be about gaining any sort of validation because that isn't needed for you to proceed and neither is understanding.

Other people's understanding and support are not required for your progress and so you, we, can't go into it thinking that way. Rather, we should share our goals to gain a sense of accountability. Allow people to have their reactions, whether they believe in you or doubt you, it sets accountability. Either you go into your goals not wanting to let someone down or not wanting someone to be right about their doubts. People-pleasing is rooted in a mindset that says "Look at me! Look what I did! Look what I'm doing! Am I good enough yet? Do you like me yet? Do you love me yet?

Does what I'm doing make you happy? Do you approve of me? Do you validate me? Am I good enough or do I need to be different? Do I need to change myself? Or am I okay?" It yanks questions out of us about whether we are currently good enough or if we need to change and let people's reactions towards us do the deciding between those two questions.

I naturally feel a need to scope out situations with new people and figure out what I can and can't be. I go through a process of analyzation based off of how they are currently interacting with me. I ask myself, almost unconsciously, "can I keep my comfortable tone of voice, or do I need to be louder? Can I let loose and enjoy myself, or do I need to drawback? Can I be my funny self, or do I need to keep it mature? Can I share my real thoughts and ideas, or would it be easier to keep quiet so I don't get dismissed and judged? Can I tell people my exciting new goals or will they think I'm obsessed with myself?"

Whether or not I shared my authentic self with people was always based on whether I thought they would judge me. And I knew it would hurt less if people judged a watered-down unauthentic version of myself rather than the real, authentic, me. If I was shy, reserved, hesitant, soft-spoken, sheepish, diffident, and timid then at least if people judged that it wasn't as bad because, at the end of the day, that's not who I am anyways. As opposed to judging me for being quirky, energized, truthful, excited, lively, futuristic, talkative, funny, and visionary because that is who I am. I know what it feels like to be judged for those things and it cuts like a knife.

So I learned to hide that part of me and keep it locked away because if people were going to get mad about those parts of me, then I just didn't want anyone to even see it until I got comfortable enough to show the authentic me. We shouldn't feel the need to keep ourselves on lockdown out of fear of making other people uncomfortable. Understand the difference between pleasing and serving. These are two very *different* things with opposite *intentions*. Pleasing is an attempt to make someone happy with you or approve of you for your feeling of security. Serving is to use your talents, time, and energy to enhance the lives or experiences of other people, generally without being asked or compensated for it.

Pleasing is for our gain, serving is for other's gain. Pleasing is about us and what we can gain, serving is about other's and what we can give. When we make the flip between pleasing and serving, we can reverse our people-pleasing tendencies. We have to reverse engineer our minds when it comes to people-pleasing. Instead of approval and recognition being the goal, switch it to something of service. When we feel tempted to compare ourselves when we feel ourselves going down the hole of inferiority when we feel like we need to prove ourselves or make others like and admire us, switch it as fast as you can to serve.

Switch your perspective from what people are thinking about you to what you can do to serve others or brighten their day. Instead, go above and beyond in your job to make it easier for someone else. Volunteer to help with certain things, buy your friend lunch, clean out the fridge for your Mom, it doesn't matter. But serving will give you that same feeling of accomplishment and impact that you desire when you're pleasing people. It will just be with better intentions.

I promise that doing nice, thoughtful things for other people is going to make them happy. And it will make you feel so good and satisfied.

It is a win-win. It is so much better than aiming to please people for your security because people liking you is not a sustainable thing you base your security off of. But when we live life with a spirit of service and giving, we are helping make other people's lives easier and more enjoyable while also getting the satisfaction of making them happy because you did something kind. And it doesn't have to be about recognition or superiority or validation, you can get the feeling you're searching for without having to feel like you're fighting for approval. People pleasing can be overcome by making a few adjustments in our lives. If you commit to adjusting and improving the way you think, the way you conduct yourself, and to swapping pleasing for serving, you will live life immensely more secure, more confident, more authentic, and more joyful because you won't be living for anyone's approval any longer.

PLAYING SMALL

Again, I wouldn't say I was bullied in school, but I remember how much people ridiculed me and nitpicked. I believe it happened most often because it was easy. It was so easy to pick on me as a kid because I just let it happen. I was so compliant and submissive to whatever people said to me or about me. It's like I would get judged for being too loud, but I would get judged for being too quiet. I'd get judged for putting myself out there and judged for being too reserved.

I don't know if you've ever heard the term "damned if you do, damned if you don't" but that was pretty much my social life... Whatever I was, I was always too much or too little. People decided that for me and I didn't exactly make it difficult for them. People love to give their opinions and criticisms and I was the kind of person who made it easy for people to do that. I was open to criticism and I was an acquiescent kid.

Meaning I was always ready to do what anybody else wanted without protest. On top of that, I was ready to *agree* with anybody about their opinions without protest. But no matter what, it always seemed like someone had a problem with me or wanted to change something about me, and they always let me know about it. If someone didn't like something about me, I didn't make it hard for them to let me know about it because I was open to receiving it. The hard part, too, is people aren't always necessarily mean or rude about their approach to criticize. Many people do it through belittling and joking.

I developed a mindset of playing small because I figured that was least likely to get any ridicule if I just kept to myself. It seemed to be the path of least resistance. People-pleasing and playing small share *many* similarities. We play small to avoid negative reactions from other people which is, what I think, the most glaring form of people-pleasing.

When we play small, it's written all over us. We keep our head down,

voice down, arms crossed. We don't make eye contact. We don't say anything that will ruffle any feathers.

We don't state what we want in a situation. We don't speak up. We are compliant, agreeable, and quiet. This was me in any social environment, any team, or any job I held. People-pleasing is nothing more than a bad habit derived from fear of getting negative reactions. It takes twenty-one days to break a bad habit or form a new habit and ninety days to form a new lifestyle. Within this book, I want to guide you towards breaking the habit of people-pleasing and forming habits that will shape you into an assertive and direct individual, instead of compliant and timid.

Here are some basic tips for overcoming people-pleasing. We will dive deeper into some of these later on, but I just want to get everything laid out on the table for you and front load the fundamentals.

1. FOCUS MORE ON YOUR ACTIONS AND LESS ON OTHER PEOPLE'S REACTIONS

When you're fully invested in what you're doing, you don't have time or energy to focus on what other people think about it. *Focus* on your "why" and your intention as much as possible, it makes it easier to overlook the temptation to play small. You'll have a different approach to what you're doing when you make it a mission. When you're on a mission, you don't look to the left or the right to see who's watching or who's judging, you're focused, eyes locked forward. Visualize that and embody it with everything you do. Become so focused and centralized on your vision that you don't feel the urge to look around to see who's watching. Become a person of intention and let your actions become the main focus instead of other people's reactions. When you're in full pursuit of you're calling, it becomes really hard to play small.

2. SAY NO, MORE

We will touch on this subject more later, but you need to know the power saying no has in your life. If you ever feel taken advantage of, it's probably because you don't exercise your power to say no nearly enough. Been there, done that. I was practically a professional "yes man." But saying yes to everything is the purest form of people-pleasing. That's because we know people will be pleased with us when we agree to their terms and agenda. It feels good when people are happy with us.

It feels good when people are contented by us agreeing to their requests. That is until you have to fulfill a commitment you didn't want to make. Next thing you know, you're backing out of plans and guilt ridden for disappointing another friend or flaking out on another plan. After all, you did say yes in the first place. But telling people no will eliminate that disaster and you'll be able to say yes to things that matter most to you. It will eliminate people who take advantage of you or your time.

You're not a doormat. You're not a yes-man. saying yes to everything takes away from your priorities, saying no puts you back in control of your time and life.

3. PERMIT YOURSELF TO LET GO OF GUILT

Guilt is such a counterproductive emotion. If you're going to make a decision that's best for you, being guilty about it completely takes away from the point. Allow yourself to go about choosing the right decisions for *your* life and eliminate guilt as much as possible. We should never feel guilty for taking care of ourselves or doing what makes us happy, never. Take a deep breath and let it go; guilt doesn't benefit anyone.

4. STOP APOLOGIZING

Get in the habit of only apologizing when you mean it. Any other time is a fake attempt at being polite. Us people-pleasers are great at apologizing for things that are not our fault. This learned habit for me came from a thought that "maybe if I say sorry, they won't be as mad at me." It is not your job to be sorry for every little inconvenience in someone else's life. You're not everyone's customer service rep. Apologies aren't something to aimlessly throw around, we say sorry when we've done something wrong when we are remorseful and to ask for forgiveness.

Nothing else. Apologizing is not a form of kindness. You can say sorry in the form of "I'm sorry for your loss" or "I'm sorry you're having a bad day" but apologizing for something you didn't have any control over does nobody any good. It's another form of people-pleasing, and it has to be unlearned.

5. TAKE TIME WHEN DECIDING TO MAKE A COMMITMENT

I have a bad habit of committing to things right away without thinking about it. This only leaves me with a full plate and very little time. It's more than okay to take a second to think before making commitments. Maybe your natural reaction is to say yes right away. But take a few minutes to assess how this commitment will affect your other priorities. This goes back to saying "no." You don't need to commit to everything and when you do, you will find it harder to exercise your right to say no. Make commitments to things most important to you and things that align with your priorities.

6. ACT THE WAY YOU WANT TO FEEL

When I speak, I speak with boldness. I'm direct with people in my conversations. I approach people with confidence. These are three powerful affirmations you can say each morning to start to shift the way you carry yourself. You must pay close attention to your posture. When you *play* small, you're also *speaking* small. You're using unsure language, second-guessing your answers, apologizing too much, asking permission too much, and speaking in a shy, soft way to avoid a negative reaction from someone.

It also results in a small bodily posture. Maybe your arms are crossed in front of your chest, shoulders are shrugged, avoiding eye contact, head down. Change your posture and body language. Have an open body posture, hold your head high and be aware of your stance. The only thing playing small ever did to me was to take away my confidence and ambition. I felt small. *All* the time. It didn't happen all at once, but I started to get tired of worrying so much about being judged, making people upset, or making other people feel bad.

I was sick of it. I have got a mission. I have a vision for my life. I have things to do. I don't have the time or desire anymore to play small so that people around me feel comfortable and don't want to judge me. That was the *most* transformative thing that happened to me. Nothing will transform your life as much as standing up, getting upset about the situation, and making a decision to change it.

It does not benefit ANYONE to play small. Read that again! Not a single person! So, stop feeling like you playing small is some form of kindness or humility towards other people because it's not. It's not humility, it's lying about who you are. It's not kindness. You get one life to live and you get to decide who you are and how you act. I know you don't want to spend it living as a watered-down version of yourself, so you don't make anyone else upset. People get upset, uncomfortable and offended over the stupidest things, I promise that your efforts to play small and please people will not change that fact. So, give it up. If you play small, you stay small.

OVERCOMING OPINIONS, ASSUMPTIONS, AND MISUNDERSTANDINGS

Because of my soft-spoken, reserved, people-pleasing tendencies, I have, more often than not, been misunderstood. We all know what it feels like to be misunderstood, it's frustrating. As a people-pleaser, it felt like I was misunderstood more often than not. People misunderstood my intentions, my words, my actions. And out of that misunderstanding came assumptions about me. So, not only is it frustrating to be misunderstood but then to have assumptions and accusations made about you from a misunderstanding? Talk about annoying.

I share this because we worry about what other people think about us so much, but this is how it starts most of the time; a misunderstanding. When people don't fully know your story or situation, they will come to conclusions on their own in their head and then try to decide your story or situation. I hated the feeling of being misunderstood because I felt like I had to explain everything I did so that everyone understood it. Even if they didn't agree. I would have, one hundred percent, rather people understood me than agree with me. So, when people misunderstood me, I felt like I had to explain myself and make people understand because I didn't want them thinking the wrong thing about me or my intentions.

Sound familiar at all? This tendency is also a form of people-pleasing and it causes us to worry way too much about what people think, know, or feel about us. What people think about us, they form opinions based on. So, as people-pleasers, we want people to think the best of us so that their opinions reflect their admiration for us. We crave admiration. So, we have discovered that misunderstandings lead to incorrect assumptions, which lead to uneducated opinions, which leads us to believe that we need to overexplain ourselves to prevent those things from happening. But even in our explanations people just won't get it. They will still misunderstand, so this whole thing is just another big crazy cycle.

And the truth is, we won't always have an opportunity to explain ourselves anyways. Someone could hear one thing about you, accurate or not and make a million different assumptions and accusations. Does that mean you need to listen? No! Does that mean their assumptions have credibility? No!

I understand the frustration of being misunderstood. Because I am more reserved, people will generally assume my intentions because I'm not always open about it. But even if I tried my best to explain myself, some people still would not get it. I think it is important to be open about our intentions, but understand that even if people know your intentions, some will still have negative thoughts towards it. You won't always get a chance to share your intentions or explain why you do what you do. Some people will just take the minuscule thing they see about you and roll with it, creating every assumption they possibly can.

So, share your intentions because it is a good thing to do. But don't do it to avoid people's bad opinions towards you because some people will have them either way. Explaining ourselves does not get us out of other people's negative feedback. A mistake we make is *over*-explaining ourselves when it's just not necessary. You don't *need* to explain yourself to anyone. There is a difference between sharing your intentions with the right people because it's the right thing to do in that situation and over-explaining so that you can wiggle your way out of any harsh opinions or misguided judgments. It's not worth it and it doesn't work most of the time. Let people think what they think.

Not everyone deserves an explanation of why you do what you do. You don't owe that to anyone. And I know it's hard because we do deeply crave to be understood, heard, and validated. People will have opinions, either way, you don't need to waste your breath trying to convince anyone to validate your decisions. What happens when people do make assumptions about you based on a complete misunderstanding of the overall, misguided interpretation of who you are? I would say brush it off, but if it was that easy this wouldn't even be a problem.

It's not that easy. For some it is. But for someone like me and my overthinking, people-pleasing habits, I needed someone to tell me how to let it go. We, as people-pleasers want people to like us and approve of us. Negative opinions are so frustrating to us because it is solid evidence of not getting what we've strived for; what we deeply desired. So, while it is important that we get over our desire to please people, it is equally important that we get over our need to know what people are thinking or saying about us.

Say it with me: it does not matter. Anyone who has time to sit around criticizing and judging other people is not very invested in their own goals or life. And if they are invested, they won't make it far because all judging and criticizing other people heavily does is increase your loneliness. So why sweat it? My two points are don't worry about someone who criticizes something they don't even understand, as well as, don't be the person who criticizes something you don't even understand. Just stay away from criticism all together as much as possible because it is such a turn-off and is not something of high character.

You must understand that the person you hope to become is going to cost you the person you are now. It's time for some transformation and I think one of the most fundamental ways to transform and get on a higher level is to stop caring what others think. People will always have something to say. You don't need me to tell you this. I know for certain that you have stories of times people judged you. You have been judged for how you look, what you wear, what decisions you make, etc., I felt the weight of opinions when I decided not to go to college after high school. Everyone had an opinion. Going back to school was the traditional thing to do. It's what all my friends were doing. I had spent the past 4 years being forced to prepare for something I knew in my heart I didn't want or need to do.

After telling someone that I had no plans for college, it was quickly met with very opinionated feedback such as, "So are you just a lazy bum?". "You'll never be successful without a college degree". "As long as you're just taking a break and you go back to school eventually, you'll be okay". "You need to go to college, it's the only way you'll make it in life." I made an intentional decision that aligned with my vision for *my* life.

I made choices accordingly. I could have gone to college just to play it safe.

I could have bought into everyone else's opinions about the correlation between success and a college degree. But I didn't and I am so happy about it. Because what a shame it would have been to have been bullied into a decision like that? Ignoring opinionated comments and sticking to what I knew was truly best for me was the greatest decision I could have made. However, this is just an example, but I know you have one of your own in the back of your mind. People will try to convince you to do things the way they've always been done. My advice? Listen to the people you admire and aspire to become. Learn to filter out opinions.

Not everyone should have a say in your life. Assess what's best for you, do your research, seek out advice from important sources, make your decision, and roll with it. I have been judged a lot for my ambition. I am extremely passionate about what I do and very serious about my goals and sometimes I can be a little intense. Even though I wouldn't even call it intense, I just call it extremely passionate. I am zealous when it comes to my dreams and goals for my future.

Many times, my strong passion has been judged, sometimes by people close to me in my life and it is such an ugly feeling. You know this feeling. So, relate your story to mine. I felt so shot down when my excitement was dismissed because of someone else's close-minded disbelief. At the time I didn't realize that's what it was. I took it very personal and it was very hurtful.

I felt like people truly didn't think I could accomplish what I had set out to and while that is still the case in some situations, it turns out that the majority of the time, people just didn't think it was a worthy enough goal or possible for anyone to achieve. It was rarely a personal thing, but I took it very personally. It made me feel like I wasn't good enough and I got so sick and tired of having exciting and exhilarating ambitions, telling people just to have them shut down or not be met with even half the excitement that I had. Now, I have been blessed with a very supportive family, but there were still encounters in my life when I shared my ambitions and they were harshly shot down. I remember when I got a new job, I was so excited about what it had to offer and the opportunity, just for it to be met with "Door to door sales? So you're one of *those* people? People never actually become successful doing that."

Or how about when I joined a network marketing company to create financial stability for myself and entrepreneurial experience as a young adult? That was often met with: "So you're a part of a pyramid scheme? So, you can make money by having slaves under you? Those things never work. You will never make it at that."

Or when I bought tickets to business training, conferences, and leadership events, to grow as an entrepreneur and learn how to become successful, that was often met with: "You're spending more money on that? You're going to another one of those? Do you even learn anything at those things? That's a waste of money" Or when I decided to pursue a startup business instead of going back to college because I am an entrepreneur and knew school was, and never had, served me or gave me the tools I needed to succeed, so I decided to pursue business and seek out more sustainable, valuable forms of education for my endeavor.

That was often met with: "So are you lazy? Do you never want to get a good job? What are you going to do to make money? You will never be successful." Or when I discovered my love and passion for traveling the world, I spent some time right after high school traveling around the country. I went to Seattle all by myself, where I learned how to catch flights, find my hotel, navigate an unfamiliar city (safely), discovered new things and new places.

I also went to multiple other states during those years. At seventeen I had only been to one other state, in three years I had traveled to twelve different states. It was an opportunity that allowed me to venture, to see God's creation, to live in the freedom I just received as a young adult after a childhood of tough responsibility, to explore around and not stay stationed in one area for the rest of my life. That was often met with: "It must be nice to take vacations all the time instead of working as a real adult." You get the point by now and I know you could sit down and write your versions of these stories.

Times when people completely misread your intentions and judged your decisions. Notice, each one of these decisions in my life was made with a lot of intentionality and boldness. People mischaracterized me for lazy, ignorant, and unsuccessful simply because they didn't understand my intentions. It happens all the time and it will continue to happen as long as you keep pushing for greatness. Also notice, nothing anybody ever said to me about those things stopped me. I still pursue my network marketing business (and I make money from it), I still invest in training and business conferences (that is where I became inspired to write this book), I still have never stepped foot on a college campus (and I've been building that photography business for four years alongside three other businesses of mine), and I still travel around the world every chance I get (and I love it).

These aren't any crazy stories of victory, we're still in the baby stages, but it's an affirmation that I was making the right decisions even when people tried to make me think I wasn't. People *will* judge what they *don't* understand. It's up to you to decide to accept it as truth or to just simply proceed with what you know you are passionate about. Either they will be right, or you will. In my situation, I was right all but one time. I did end up quitting my sales job, but I kept pushing when people around me told me to quit. I had a lot of faith in my vision with that job, ultimately, total burn out is what led me to quit.

But I knew that at the end of the day, it had to be completely my decision to quit and not just because people were telling me to because of their lack of faith or because of their fear. I understand it coming from a place of love when people tell you not to do something. But you have to decide what to do because you can't let other people's judgments, loving or not, keep you held back all your life. You have to make decisions to move forward with your passions even when it doesn't make sense to anyone but you. Let people think you're crazy for a while, it's fun. But be so committed to your follow-through that in five years you can look back and have little stories of victory.

Whether they worked out or not, whether they were successful or not, if you decided to go for it, that is a victory because that's not something many people do these days. Sadly, people remain held back in fear of judgment and they look back with regret. I have a story like that. When I was fifteen, I started taking dance classes. I had already decided two years prior that I wanted to be a dancer-it was just a matter of waiting for the right time to be able to start taking classes. I trained on my own until that day, and when I started actual classes, the dream was only confirmed. I knew I was a dancer at heart, this was my dream. I practically lived at the studio every evening and on weekends.

I took every class I possibly could, I danced on the competitive team, I was training for a duet and a solo for competitions. I quickly got into teaching. I taught classes for four hours straight two nights a week plus additional classes and rehearsals that lasted from 7:30 in the morning until 6:00 PM. Eventually, as a teacher at the studio, I got my key so I would stay for hours later practicing and just living my craft. I went to as many conventions as I could, I traveled to California to compete my solo, I found that I was so challenged and so fulfilled. I was the happiest because I was so involved in my passion and because I fulfilled the promise to myself that I would be a dancer one day. Just like everything we are passionate about, people will put in their opinions about it and that is what happened to me.

I started feeling like I couldn't pursue dance. I was an adult now, I needed to find a reliable source of income. I also came to the harsh reality of how nearly impossible it was to become a professional dancer that made even a decent income. I had just turned eighteen and the pressure to get my life together was too much. The pressure I put on myself and pressure from outside sources telling me that dance wasn't enough, and I'd have to find some other interests if I ever wanted to make money. It was all hitting me at once and I gave in. The limitations became too much and other people's disbelief became my own.

Other factors played a role in my decision, but ultimately, I could have decided to push through and treasure what I had worked so hard to create for myself. I didn't and part of me knows I was just trying to make a good decision for myself and my future but the other part of me regrets leaving my dream like that. The regret stings. It does. But the good news is you can restart at any time and choose to do things differently. You can choose to push through judgment and go into it with full, pure authenticity and be your true self this time. You can choose to not feel weighed down by what people think or what people will say.

It doesn't matter, if it has tugged on your heart this much to even be thinking about it years after you've given up, that's a huge sign you should continue to pursue it. You can always start over. You can always do it differently. It doesn't have to be the same story this time, it can be better. You have permission to make it better. Make things right with yourself and do what it's longing for you to do. Because I allowed people's judgment in, I spent years in timid inaction. I allowed other people's opinions to take away my dream.

You *need* to make an active decision to stop being addicted to the approval of others. *YOU* get to choose who you listen to and who you don't. You get to choose whose opinions have a say and who you allow having a place in your life. I've had to make the decision that some people's opinions about me were not grounded in anything, they were uninformed, and although people are entitled to their opinions, I'm not entitled to accept them as truth or comply with them. I choose who I listen to and who I don't. If outside validation is the only source of your nourishment, you will starve your whole life.

Validation is a moving target. I used to care a lot about what people thought about me or said about me. And it took me a lot of work to develop this mindset, but now I do my best not to feed any attention to the ridiculous opinions of other people. If you place your entire source of validation on the shoulders of one person, there *will* come a day when they tell you that you *can't* do something and you will believe them. They will tell you that you can't.

They will tell you to quit or do it differently. *Do not claim someone else's disbelief as your own.* Make up your mind about what you believe and let people have their opinions about it. You're not obligated to listen to it. I don't care if it's your Mom or your best friend, your sister, your teacher, your Dad, or anyone for that matter. God has given each of us a unique calling in our lives. Our missions will always be different from the next persons.

So, someone who doesn't understand it or is scared will try to talk you out of it. And even if it's from a place of love, it's an *opinion*. A lot of people will try to talk you out of things they had a bad experience with. Of course, there is so much value in listening to people trying to protect you. But also understand that nobody knows you're vision like you do. God has given you a purpose. Don't let someone else talk you out of it because of their fear and disbelief.

Own that. Trust God. We are more than conquerors with Him: I know it's not easy to let go of other people's opinions; it's something I battled with for a long time- it's a muscle that needs to be strengthened. You are not here just to cater to the opinions of other people. I want to show you how you can let go of the weight of opinions and have more freedom in your life.

1. **CHOOSE TO LISTEN TO PEOPLE WHO HAVE ALREADY DONE WHAT YOU WANT TO**

One thing that has helped me so much through this process is the realization that if someone is placing an opinion on me and they haven't even done what I'm aspiring to do then their opinion doesn't have much grounding. If I'm trying to write a book, I'm not going to listen to the opinions of someone who has never kept a journal, let alone written a book. If I want to become a millionaire, I'm going to go and learn from millionaires, not college professors. I wouldn't go and get marriage counseling from someone whose never been married. You get the point. If you haven't done it, don't try to tell me how to do it. You must weed out some opinions.

Choose what matters most and prioritize that. Remember when we talked about how easy making opinions are? Anyone on God's green earth can do it. It's not hard to form an opinion about someone. You deserve better than to give so much credit to so many random opinions. You *don't* have to listen to everyone and that's the bottom line. You get to pick and choose. So do so. If someone's opinion doesn't correspond with your vision then you, and I know this will sound crazy, need to let it go.

I know that people will have their opinions and at the end of the day, it's none of my business. I don't have to listen to it; my goal is not to change anyone's mind. People love to have an opinion about everything. They love it. I don't do what I do to serve people who have a negative outlook on my work. I don't do it for the haters. So why would I allow the sudden care about what they think about me or what I do?

I'm not doing it for them.

You need to get good at filtering out opinions. You may say you don't care about other people's opinions but as soon as someone says something negative, false, nasty, or uninformed about you, you go around thinking about it all day. That's caring. Truly not caring means letting it go right away. It means choosing to tune out gossip. It means not needing to know what so-and-so said about you. If it's truly irrelevant to your happiness and success, which it should be, then it shouldn't be hard to tune out the nonsense.

Not everyone's opinions deserve space in your heart or your mind. Then you have no space for opinions that matter; opinions that might protect you or help you make better decisions. Filtering out opinions is not something that happens overnight. *Especially* if you're a people-pleaser. As people-pleasers, we almost feel a sense of obligation when it comes to the opinions people place on us. We feel obligated to listen to them. We feel as though we are being polite when we comply with people's opinions about us.

You must begin analyzing every opinion and deciding whether it corresponds with your intention or who you are as a person. If its incorrect, hurtful, unhelpful, disrespectful, uninformed, petty, rude, or ignorant, it needs to be filtered out. That means you brush it off instantly. You don't think about it for a second longer. That takes practice, but you've got to start.

I used to think that not listening to the opinion of others was me disrespecting them which was a total excuse to let people walk all over me. I'm a child of God, thank you. If you're not Him and I didn't ask for your opinion, it will be voided. When you accept everyone's opinions as truth; when you allow opinions to be your validation, it leaves so much room for doubt and overthinking. I've always believed I had an overthinking problem but really, I just had an approval-seeking problem. It's taken a lot of practice and it's something I'm still working on.

But there's simply not space for everyone to have an opinion in my life. And honestly, if you aren't in the game with me, you don't get an opinion. If you aren't walking alongside me in my life, if you don't see how hard I work, if you don't know what I've been through, if you don't know my heart or my vision or my intention, you don't get a say. It's a privilege to have my acceptance of your opinion. That's just my attitude about it and it allowed me to walk in such freedom not having to take everyone's negativity personally knowing that I'm in control and I don't need to listen to everyone's feedback about my life has been freeing. A weight will be lifted off your back when you stop placing value on everyone's opinions- embrace that attitude, and you will be transformed.

2. HAVE THE CONFIDENCE TO DEAL WITH OTHER PEOPLE'S OPINION'S

Work on your communication skills. You MUST start being more direct with people. When my confidence level raised, my attitude was sharper, I was more direct with people. Understand that gossip does not come from a place of maturity. I'd go as far as to say that gossip and nasty opinions are a huge indicator of underperformers. At the end of the day, you should be so focused on your own goals and vision rather than being worried about what people are saying about it.

We can't feel like giving up every time others don't see the value in what we're pursuing because the tough truth is that a lot of people won't. You've got to take the punches and roll with it. Most of the people you are friends with now won't be in your life when you're on your death bed. Stop making decisions based on other people's opinions. It's robbing you of your legacy.

If you listened to everyone's opinions on what you should be doing, where you should live, how you should make money, what you should study in school, where would you be? Honestly ask yourself and envision the person you would be if you listened to all the opinions. I'll do it too. If I listened to everyone's opinions, I would be in tens of thousands of dollars deep in student loan debt, I would have never taken a trip out of the country, I would have no tattoos, I'd still live at home, I wouldn't have my travel club or all the friends I've made within the club and without that business, I would have no plan for financial stability.

I'd take the person I am today over that person every time.

When you buy someone's opinion, you buy their lifestyle. If you don't want what someone has then why would you listen to how they tell you to do things? Figure out what is important to you and get good at filtering out opinions that don't help you improve or get closer to your goals.

BECOMING MORE ASSERTIVE

The problem with being overly complaint is that it's so visually apparent. People can sense insecurity and a closed-off demeanor from miles away. And it opens the door. Unfortunately, the thing we do to avoid judgment and criticism opens the door for so much uninvited criticism. It opens the door for people to treat you poorly because the way you're conducting yourself shows that you're not going to do anything about it. Playing small is an open door for people to treat you however they want.

I am convinced that the primary reason I was talked down to or verbally disrespected by people is because I played small and that showed people that I wouldn't do anything about it. People sensed a lot of ease with treating me however they pleased because I demonstrated my compliance and willingness to receive it instead of calling out what was wrong in the way people communicated with me. My people-pleasing conduct sent out the message loud and clear that "I'm shy, I'm polite, I won't talk back, you can say whatever you'd like, you can disrespect me and I won't say anything about it.

You can yell at me or cuss at me or talk to me as though I'm inferior and I will comply." My fear of confrontation and command for mutual respect turned me into that person. I could sit here for hours listing off all the jobs whom the leader, manager, higher-up, instead of teaching me with respect and decency, snapped at me, dismissed me, yelled at me, and insulted me while I was trying to learn a new job. You might be thinking what a softy I am for letting bad bosses hurt my feelings like this. I understand how common it is to work for poor leaders; my situation was far from the worst. These are the stories that led to my people-pleasing, however, fear of confrontation led to compliance in the way people talked to me because a part of me would have rather let people lash out at me and get it all out and be done than to be the person who

stood up for myself and risked worse reactions. I wasn't the kind of person who demanded respect with the way I conducted myself.

I wasn't confident, I wasn't assertive. I wasn't direct. So, people didn't need to treat me decently if they didn't want to. There is nothing respectful or polite about allowing people to be rude. People in this world will be rude, we don't need to be soft-skinned, that is not what I'm getting at. But the people you do business with, your clients, your customers, your colleagues, your family members, anybody you work with closely or spend significant time with should not get off with insulting, belittling, diminishing, or disrespecting you. I needed someone to tell me I had permission to stand up for myself. That accepting people's poor attempt at superiority wasn't a sign of respect.

Maybe you need to hear that same thing and I'm here to deliver the message: you are not a doormat for everyone to walk all over- respect does not equal the allowance of people to control you with lashing out. People want control and that's the bottom line. People love to be in control of situations, they love to feel superior. This desire, when not handled correctly, results in arrogance and haughty condescension. Maybe your opinions, thoughts or feelings have been shut down regularly. Maybe you've become so scared of angry, condescending people that your reaction is to remain the punching bag to not risk further ridicule.

If you're anything like me, when I get emotional or angry, words escape my mind. I can't think of what to say or how to respond. So, I lived in fear of confronting people because I always knew that if they struck back at me, I'd be done for. I'd be toast because I hadn't practiced standing up for myself or commanding respect. Maybe you think it's easier to just shut up and let everyone else do the talking and decision making because you don't like conflict. But being compliant just to serve everyone else's need for control is not beneficial in any sense.

Giving up control to avoid conflict won't *serve* you, it will *deplete* you. You have a voice, your thoughts matter, you're deserving of mutual respect amongst people you work closely with. If you have ever had a customer service roll in your life, you know how strongly this struggle can be applied in this situation. I have worked nothing but customer service jobs and have encountered some of the nastiest people. There is a fine line between doing your job and conducting yourself as a person who will be treated with respect as long as you're doing business together. My attitude needed a huge change.

I had to learn to command respect with a smile on my face and utmost kindness. There *is* a balance between being kind and serving, as well as, being a person who doesn't receive poor treatment. I know it can be tricky in situations like this, but you do not have to let people treat you like crap in your job. What helped me was knowing my job extremely well so that when customers got snooty or wanted to take control, I could make decisions in direct alignment with what was right. The antidote to condescending behavior is direct, confident communication. You do not have to allow anybody to talk down to you or belittle you.

But it is up to you to be the kind of person who conducts themselves as confident and direct. If you don't believe you're worthy of being treated respectfully, go back to the identity chapter. Remember how God views you and how he thinks of you. You have the right to stand up for yourself. You have the right to refuse to comply with patronizing conduct from people around you. So how do we accomplish this? By mastering the way, we approach and communicate with people.

I will write a whole chapter about language, but *how* we speak is just as important as *what* we speak. The *way* you speak needs to reflect the confident, sure person you are becoming. The way to become the person you are aspiring to is to act like that person each day. When you think of your best self, how does that person talk to people? How does that person speak and interact with people? How does that person conduct themselves? Sometimes nothing crazy needs to happen for you to become that person, you just have to start showing up as them daily.

I don't know about you, but I have a really hard time forming the right words to say on the spot. But I knew that I wanted the way I spoke to people and approached people to reflect the confident, bold woman I was becoming. It's something that takes practice but that's how you become that person. You must send out the right signals. Show people through your direct and assertive conduct that you are confident and secure in yourself and your decisions. When you speak as though you're unsure, that is exactly how people will treat you. That sends out the message that you need coaching or bossing around. I want to encourage you to be more direct in your conversations and watch the way people start to treat you differently.

Here are some examples of compliant, people-pleasing statements that you *can* swap for more direct and assertive, grounded statements: "Can you fill out this form for your appointment, if you don't mind? Can be swapped to: "Before you can be seen, we will need this form filled out. The pens are right here, thank you!" Turn your questions into bold statements of assurance.

No doubt being polite is important and it goes a long way. But we can be polite and direct at the same time; I know how frustrating it can be being in a group of outgoing people- being confident and bold when you're someone who is reserved and soft-spoken is challenging. But the mistake we make is thinking that our words don't matter as much. So, we stay quiet and let the outgoing people do the talking. Whether you're a loud, fun outgoing, the life of the party kind of person, or a laid back, reticent person, not one type of person is more allowed to speak freely.

I will say that being more outgoing will definitely make your voice heard, however, I oftentimes just didn't talk because I would leave it to the outgoing people. *Allow* yourself to be involved in conversations. You don't need to just sit back and observe conversations with people, you *can* participate. You don't have to observe fun, community, parties, friend groups, you can be involved in them. Becoming more assertive opened more doors for me. Not only was being direct important in my job, but it had and has the same importance in my everyday life.

Success belongs to those who get up and *take* it. Not those who sit back and wait for it to be handed to them or those who ask permission before taking action. Be direct in what you want, know what you want, and get up and take it. Refuse to be refused. Have diligence and persistence. I believe that this is how we achieve our goals. It will make your work life better because your clients or customers will respect your assertiveness. They will look at you as a person who knows what they are talking about and that creates respect.

It will eliminate the situations that you get taken advantage of because you will represent yourself as someone who doesn't mess around with people who walk all over you. It will *decrease* situations where people feel the need to boss you around because you're direct conduct will demonstrate your ability to communicate clearly. It will increase your confidence and make you more respectable. The great thing about becoming more direct is that is doesn't come at the cost of your kindness.

You *can* do everything I just mentioned, and be the kindest person in the world at the same time. Direct language *does not* come at the cost of kindness. You do not have to forfeit your soft heart, your smile, or your kind words to be more direct with people in conversation. I would implore you to have both of these characteristics. Be direct with people, communicate clearly. But do so with a smile on your face and kindness in your heart.

OVER COMING SELF-LIMITING BELIEFS

For me, my self-limiting mindset was rooted in a belief that if I tore myself down first, nobody else could make me feel worse. This tied into people-pleasing in the sense that I always knew in my heart that people would judge me for who I was, so I would just judge myself first to relieve the sting. It used to take me a very long time to truly be myself around new people because I had conditioned my mind to play safe by playing small. Somewhere along the way, I learned that if I am always playing small, if I'm always keeping to myself and never sharing my true thoughts if I'm never being my authentic self, then when people judge me, they're not judging the real, authentic me and that will keep me safe.

I remember so many times speaking out about what I wanted, sharing my true thoughts just to have them shut down and just to be ridiculed. It put up barriers in my heart and mind. It hurt me as a little girl and as a young woman when I was just being me and someone else hated it so much, they had to tear me down for it. I took things way too personal way too often in my life, and it caused me to live extremely reserved to avoid the judgment of who I truly was and I put limitations in my mind, insults, and belittlements before anyone else could so that in a way I was prepared for that feedback and it didn't hurt as much because I already knew.

I felt like I was preparing for what people would judge me for by judging myself first- by planting seeds of limiting thoughts in my mind. I also let the enemy have his way in my mind far too many times. The mind is a very tricky place. It is so easy to overthink yourself into a downward spiral. It's easy to let the enemy influence your thought process. He has your insecurities to play off of, and it's not like you can

deny those insecurities exist, so you believe whatever lies he plants in your mind. Even worse, you build off of it.

You validate what the enemy says about you by agreeing and complying. I'd say most of us deal with this. It's just become so normalized that we accept that way of thinking. We use our insecurities as limitations in our minds. We constantly downplay our potential, point out all the reasons we're not good enough.

For me, it started as a fear of being judged and so if I put limitations on myself and judged myself first, then when someone else did it, it was okay because I wasn't too sure about it either. It's like saying "I'm going to run a marathon" followed by "Probably not, honestly but maybe" as a downplay so when someone says, "Yeah right that's stupid" you can say, "Yeah exactly, you're right how dumb was that idea" as kind of a, "Get out of looking irrational for your ambitions" free card. We downplay ourselves in our approach to share our thoughts or ideas so when someone judges or offers unwelcome criticism, it's easier to deal with because we can just agree with them and move on.

In a way, we think that's easier, so we don't have to deal with people's fixed mindset judgments towards us. Which is completely understandable. I hate when I have something exciting I want to do and people around me tell me how I can't or shouldn't do it. But that way of approaching your ideas and sharing them with others is completely destructive because you're putting yourself down and throwing your ambitions in the trash before you've even spoken a word about them. How can that be a good way of thinking when going into an exciting new venture? Here is my example: when I would tell someone that I was writing this book, at first, I would play small.

I would say something like, "Yeah, I'm writing a book. We'll see how it goes, I'm not a great writer so I might not get it published." In the back of my mind, that was me not acting too serious about it, so I didn't get hit as hard with judgment and criticism. I put limiting beliefs in my mind first before I shared it with anyone. If you want to do some thing and it's come far enough for you to even want to share it with anyone, it's important to you and it's a desire of yours for a reason. You shouldn't put so many limitations and ridicule on yourself just so that if someone else doesn't agree with it, you can get out of looking bad for having "wild" dreams. If you're not ready to tell people with confidence about your plans and brush off their comments and judgments and not let it change your heart, you need to keep it in until you are *ready* to do that.

It's okay to just foster your dreams in your heart, keep them between you and God until you're ready to share them with confidence, enthusiasm, assurance, and boldness. That is the posture you deserve to have when you share your aspirations. People will offer unwelcome criticism when you share your goals, inevitably. But you have to be grounded in your decisions, confident in your choices, and ready to brush off criticism. Your limitations begin and end in your mind and it's time to tackle the self-limiting beliefs that have been holding you back for so long.

I'd like to introduce you to Karen. Karen is the voice in the back of my head that goes on and on about what I can't do. "Who do you think you are? You can't write a book. Nobody is going to read a book written by a dumb twenty-year-old. You're an imposter, all your dreams have already been accomplished by other people. You're nothing special. You don't have what it takes.

Mediocrity is all you will achieve, you have already failed at everything else, why would you succeed at this?". Maybe this sounds all too familiar to you. Our minds are a powerful thing and when we believe those thoughts, they become our reality. We have got to start getting picky about the voices we choose to listen to. And this starts with the voices in our heads.

We must retrain our subconscious minds before we can consciously choose the people we listen to. When we're filled with so much doubt and self-limiting beliefs like what you just read, we will fall for anything people say to us. Because in reality, you're already doubting yourself in your mind, so when someone comes along and discourages you for your goals or tells you what you should be doing instead, you *will* believe them. You will believe people who never had the right or the place to be telling you anything about your decisions in the first place. What we believe to be true in our minds and what we believe to be true in reality go hand in hand, but it starts with your mind.

Whether you think you can, or you can't, you're right. As cliché as it is, its 100% truth. There have been done studies on the power of belief; people have believed their way out of illnesses. Have you ever heard of the placebo effect: taking a placebo pill for illness and *believing* it would heal your sickness and it did? That just goes to show how powerful the beliefs we foster in our minds are. Match a strong, relentless belief with persistent action and friend, you will be unstoppable.

71

But that's not all that easy, is it? It's quite hard. When you're filled with doubt and insecurity all day every day, how do you just one day up and believe that you're capable when your mind keeps telling you that you're not good enough? Man, this hits my heart because I struggled with this so much. And it makes me sad to look back on what I missed out on because of my limiting beliefs about myself. If I can help even one person to have a stronger belief in themselves and more importantly, a stronger belief in the power of our awesome God, that would just be the most rewarding feeling.

As I'm writing these very words, I am consumed with self-limiting thoughts, doubt, and insecurity. But I'm doing it anyway. That's how I overcome it, by just doing it anyway. You can allow the voice in your head to shut down your ambitions, or you can push past and do it anyways. There is no magic pill we can take to get rid of self-limiting beliefs, it's not a cold. But learning how to overcome the self-sabotaging thoughts running rampant in our heads is a very significant accomplishment. We are fully capable of overcoming our self-limiting thoughts and here is how:

MAKE UP YOUR MIND.

Most of the time, the self-doubting voices in the back of your head are subconscious thoughts, which means you don't control when you think self-limiting thoughts. What we need to do here is retrain our subconscious mind; make up your mind. Because our brains are like muscles, we need to train that muscle and make it stronger every day.

PRACTICE:

Here's an exercise for you to do to start retraining your brain. Set a timer for 1 minute and write down every self-limiting thought that pops into your mind. What comes to mind when you think about going after your goals? What scares you? Acknowledge and write down every thought that floods in. After one minute is up, you're going to go back and change the narrative. So If my thought was "You fail at everything else, why would you succeed at this?" My new narrative would be something like this: "The things I have failed at before have only led me to a new and bigger level with a new ambition". Here's another one: "You're an imposter" can be switched to: "I am inspired by others who have already accomplished what I hope to one day, but that's only the beginning of what I will achieve."

Your beliefs are powerful. What you believe about yourself and your capabilities is powerful. I don't believe we will ever fully get rid of self-limiting beliefs because of its human nature. We all have a Karen. But you can overcome those beliefs and train your brain to believe powerful thoughts. Again, your brain is just like a muscle. And just like you don't go to the gym one day and come home with 6 pack abs, you can't expect to have one positive thought and just fully get rid of any negativity lurking around in your brain. You must consistently work at it. Just like working out and getting physically healthy, you have to detox your brain and start strengthening your thought process. One of the best ways to do this is through affirmations. This has become very popular amongst our society, but I'm just here to tell you that it works. For me personally, it has helped shift my mentality, and I encourage you to do it.

PART TWO:
TAKING OWNERSHIP OF YOUR LIFE

SETTING BOUNDARIES

Never underestimate the importance of setting boundaries in your life. Having no boundaries often leads to manipulation. It opens the door for people to take advantage of you. I know that anytime I felt like I was being taken advantage of, it was simply because I wasn't saying no or setting boundaries. We hold the power to allow or deny access to people. Often we just don't use that power, it all boils down to people-pleasing. But if everything I talked about in the previous chapters was meaningful, then this has to be applied with that knowledge. We have to learn to set boundaries. As a people-pleaser, I have said yes to things I didn't just to make someone else happy.

Does this sound like you? Saying no was (and sometimes still is) so incredibly hard for me to do. And when I would say no, I'd make a lame excuse that made it sound like I wanted to but just couldn't which wasn't helpful. I believe failing to tell people no is one of the biggest struggles of a people-pleaser. *Nobody* likes being told no. For a long time, I would rather have someone be happy with me than inconvenienced by my telling them no. That caused me to get taken advantage of simply because I wouldn't say no. You could count on me always saying yes to favors because I didn't want to disappoint anyone. People-pleasers are known for being "yes men". Because "yes" is far easier than someone being disappointed with you.

Until it's not. Any time I said yes to something just to please someone, it took away from other priorities in my life. But I had to realize that it was up to me to say no because as long as I kept being the "yes man" to people, the more people could push me into doing what they wanted. The more people could manipulate me. I know how hard saying no can be when you're a people-pleaser. If it was easy, obviously we wouldn't have this issue. The mindset we get stuck in is that we owe it to people to say yes to them, *especially* with close family and friends.

It is extremely challenging to tell those closest to you that you cannot help them out. I'm all for giving and being a servant leader; I believe one of the most important qualities we can have is a heart to give back to people. So don't get rid of your giving nature, that is not at all the goal here. The goal is to stop saying yes to every little favor, invite, proposal, or request that anyone brings into your space. You are *not* obligated to tell anyone, yes and that was my biggest problem. I felt extremely obligated to tell people yes. What's worse is that anytime I did say no, I spent the rest of the day feeling guilty about it.

Good ole' people-pleasing. The ultimate truth is that as long as you make everyone else's random requests a priority over your priorities, you are simply just an errand-runner. You will not have time for your own life and goals as long as you always say yes to everyone else. Saying no is an important part of prioritization. How can you possibly prioritize your goals when you're filling up your schedule with other people's agenda? I hit my breaking point a few months ago.

I said yes way more than I should have. I had my own goals and priorities, but I would say yes to coffee meetings that I didn't have time for. I would say yes to weekly commitments that went *way* later than I was prepared for. I said yes to driving places I didn't have the gas for. I said yes to spending money I didn't have on, things I didn't want. I hate having my time wasted almost more than anything else. It's up there with my hatred of hearing people chew their food.

That's when I realized that as long as I continued to say yes to everything, the more people would continue to waste my time. I had to start choosing who I said yes to and keeping my priorities first. Because if I can't show up for myself and my priorities, there's no way I can show up for anyone else. And what did saying yes to all those random things get me exactly? Nothing but a full schedule of other people's agendas. It didn't do anyone any favors because I said yes just to be nice so people thought I was interested in something that I wasn't.

I'm telling you right now, it's so much easier to say no to things than to pretend and have to go through all of this. I got sick of people wasting my time and I had to start saying no. Your time will never be your own if you keep handing it out freely. I want to teach you some things that helped me start to say no and become more intentional with who I give my time to. When we stop saying yes to things that aren't a priority, we can start saying yes to things that are.

In the time that I spent listening to other people try to talk me into joining their business, I could have been building my own. That's a hard pill to swallow. The money I spent on stupid face gel at the mall was money I could have spent on getting the computer I wanted. The lady was really sweet to me and I wanted to be nice to her so I gave her $99. I can't even believe myself. If I ever do something like that again, you have complete permission to smack me. If I wanted to give money to be "nice" I should have given to my church, or a homeless person or like a million other better things than that dumb face gel THAT DIDN'T EVEN WORK.

But the past is the past. The important thing is that I realized how unhealthy saying yes to everything is and I hope my stories will encourage you to say no more often and avoid having your time and money wasted. If you've already done what I've done, there's hope for you. It just requires saying no.

Now, each of these things individually isn't a big deal. I got over getting home late one night because of that meeting or using the rest of my gas to help my dad out by picking up my brother. But when it's multiple times that something like that happens in one week, there is an issue. An issue called being a yes man. It frustrated me so much how full my schedule was running around meeting everyone else's desires and fulfilling everyone else's requests. So I laid out the foundational things in my schedule- things like work, downtime, business work, sleeping, and spending time with my boyfriend.

Then, I assessed how much free time I had leftover and made sure I had enough time to myself. I then made sure I had plenty of space to plan time with my family, and with these priorities in place, THEN I would assess whether or not I could say yes to someone's request to meet or help them out with a project or errand. These are my priorities and we all have them. You need to lay out your most important priorities so that you know, in the first place what you even can or can't say yes to. I didn't understand my priorities or have a good grip on my schedule, so I didn't understand what I could or couldn't say yes to. I just said yes to it all.

Now here's the part where you have to say the word no. I'm smiling while writing this because it seems so simple but

78

I remember going on YouTube to get advice for saying no because I was so terrible at it and so nervous about making people disappointed. There are *two* rules when it comes to saying no; don't overexplain yourself and you must remove "I'm sorry" from your vocabulary. The *first* rule is: you don't need to explain why your telling someone no like when you're calling in sick to work. It doesn't matter.

Someone else decided to bring this request into your space, you don't need to explain why you don't want to do it. When you explain too much like, "I'm just too busy right now" or "I have the kids tonight" they will ask again when you're not busy or when you don't have the kids. Stop explaining so much and just say no. People will appreciate your direct honesty. And yes, saying no will disappoint some people. The *second* rule is to stop saying sorry! You must stop saying sorry for saying no, you're not sorry because now you can prioritize your own life above someone else's sudden requests. Whatever you do, don't say sorry. You're allowed to tell people no. You're allowed to not make any commitments. You're allowed to choose yourself. You're allowed to put your life and goals above others.

That way you have time for helping people and saying yes to things that matter. Say no and don't say sorry about it. At the end of the day, this will only make people realize that you mean business, you respect your time, therefore, they will respect you. When you set higher standards, people will know that you don't just give away your time for free and any time you agree to give to someone or something outside of your priorities is a privilege. Don't be afraid to have high standards. Respect your time and other people will start to respect it as well. Saying no was one of the hardest things for me to start doing, but it also provided me with the *most* freedom.

RISING ABOVE YOUR PAST

I had a tough childhood. I shuffled around a lot when it came to sharing my story. But I realized what the impact of sharing my story would have on me and those around me, which made my choice abundantly clear, and at that moment, I knew that getting this book and my testimony out into the world would become my top priority. It's never been easy for me to share my story because it's still so fresh and I don't want to paint a bad picture of anyone. I want to start by saying that I was raised by two hardworking parents who fought like hell to provide for my siblings and I.

My parents have never left me, they gave me love, and they gave it everything they had. That is so much more than a lot of people can say. I love my parents. They have always been there for me. But I guess you could say that life dealt my family some tough cards. My family was always under attack by the enemy. He attacked our relationships, our health, our finances, and we, as a family, went through a lot of really hard things.

It started with violent fighting that left me shaking in terror, every night for eleven years straight. It left me wondering if they would take it too far one night and I'd have one less parent to grow up with. That was a legitimate fear of mine as a little girl. The crippling fear I had all those years when my parents fought was, and still is indescribable. I sat in my bed every night, plugging my ears, shaking, crying, begging God to make it stop. To make them stop fighting. I spent every night of my life fearing that I wouldn't have a mom to grow up with. I thought I would lose both of my parents. I was terrified and it traumatized me.

I knew about the effects of alcohol addiction before I even know what alcohol was. I got a front-row seat to the disaster it creates. When my parents told us they were getting a divorce, my poor brothers and sisters were heartbroken but in my head, I thought to myself, "Please be serious this time." Is that terrible? But I just knew my parents weren't healthy together. I wanted this. I prayed for this. I wished for this on every birthday when I blew out my candles. And at that moment, my prayer was answered.

No kid wishes that their parents would divorce; it's completely unnatural.

But thinking my parents were going to severely hurt each other every day took such a toll on my heart and mental state. I've experienced years of emotional pain, trauma, darkness, fear, loss, and depression. For a long time, it was hard for me to find an ounce of good in what I had to go through as a child. I was never really able to process the effects of those things. Maybe one day I will share my whole story and write a book specifically geared towards healing from trauma, but I'm just not ready to share the depth of my past yet. But I do know the power in sharing our testimony and I want to share parts with you so that you understand the place I'm coming from.

From the time I was about nine years old, a large portion of my childhood was spent watching my brothers and sisters. I'm the oldest of seven kids so I spent a lot of time babysitting. Both of my parents worked jobs to make sure us kids had food, clothes, a home, and a good life. That's just how it is for most people these days, both parents must work to make ends meet *especially* when you're single parents to six kids. So they worked. Daycare was and is a whole other level of expensive, so I was next in line to take care of the kids.

I watched them after school, late at night, every summer, cooked them dinner, often put them to bed, walked us to the bus in the morning, etc.. It was just how life was and it's not uncommon to be the babysitter or have extra responsibility when you're the oldest in the family. But I just had *a lot* of expectation placed on me to raise these kids part-time, and full time during summer breaks. I don't know if you've spent a lot of time with kids, but they are a lot to handle. And I mean A LOT.

They are chaotic and very overwhelming. It was a lot of weight on my shoulders that I didn't know how to handle. New mothers struggle with figuring out how to care for a little human and here I was at thirteen trying to figure out how to take care of six. It was hard and too much sometimes. I took care of them so much so, that when my parents came home from work, I was drained. Kids are not easy. Especially when they're your brothers and sisters because who wants to listen to their older sister boss them around all day every day? I didn't know how to be a good caregiver to my siblings. I was bossy, I was so emotionally drained, and overwhelmed from taking care of a bunch of kids who weren't mine to care for.

When my parents would get home all I wanted was to go to my room, lay face down on my bed, scream, maybe cry, but ultimately just be alone. I wanted to be alone because I was *so* drained. But then there was this other expectation on me to spend time with my family and help with dinner and cleaning and chores. Anytime my dad saw me, I was irritable and wanted to be left alone- which sounds like a teenager thing to say, which is why I respected his intention to want me involved in the family.

But in reality, it was just me being exhausted and kind of sad. I didn't know where or what the balance was, I didn't know how to be a part-time parent to my siblings and also just be their *sister*. I felt guilty because I would get so mad at them and I didn't treat them very well at all. They probably thought I hated them and I didn't- I just resented the situation I was put in and that resentment rubbed off on them. I think bossing them around all the time made them resentful too. I know I'd hate it if my sister bossed me around all the time. So I get it. But I never got too close to them because I didn't know how to just be their sister. It had a way of making me naturally bossy but was quickly told to back off when I treated my siblings the only way I knew how It was so hard to have a relationship with them. It was a weight that shouldn't have been placed on me. I didn't know how to be their sister, and at the same time, I didn't know how to be a kid. I got so accustomed to being left in charge and left with responsibility- I couldn't just go off and play with my friends, someone had to stay home and watch the kids. I felt like I was robbed of my childhood- It affects me to this day and hinders me from letting go around people. It's hard for me to just have fun in situations that *should* be fun.

I drawback and don't let loose. I'm used to being the responsible one. Making sure everyone is taken care of and nobody gets hurt. I'm sure a lot of people think I'm weird when I act so uptight and distant when I should be having fun and acting my age. But I don't know what it means to act my age because, from such a young age, I had to behave older than I was. This experience demanded me to grow up fast. Being in charge of six kids and having to make sure they're fed and that nobody electrocuted themselves in the outlets, or ran into the street while playing outside, or colored on the walls with Sharpie, or busted their head open on the fireplace, or choked on a piece of meat that was too big, or anything. That experience *demanded* that I rise up and mature.

After all, I was in charge of the safety and well-being of six kids, acting like they were wasted on a case of Red Bulls, who did NOT want to be told what to do by me. I laugh as I write this because most of my siblings are teenagers now (some, almost adults) and they're much more fun, I was irritated, angry, and not fun to be around in any way shape or form. I have watched my dad fight through anxiety and depression. I've sat at his bedside while he had anxiety attacks. I've witnessed the horrific effects of deep depression and grief on someone I love more than anyone. But my dad has fought to give us better, he has never given up, and he always reminds us how much he loves us. I'm so grateful to have a dad in my life who loves and supports me. Through all the hardship, I can stand here and say I have a loving father in my life. I wish more people could say that. I've watched my mother be abused and mistreated. I've watched the way a man, who didn't deserve her, hatefully deceive her.

I saw the impact it had on her when she was abused, left, cheated on, disrespected, belittled, and dishonored by person after person. My mother is *the* strongest woman I know because even when her heart was being broken and she was being hurt, she continued to show up well for her children. She never threw in the towel, she invested in her health and healing which is the best thing we could have witnessed while growing up. She was mothering six kids without having had a great example of her own. I find myself taken back just by how strong she is, and was.

The things I had to do and the things I had to see, left a heavy burden on me that I carried. I wasn't joking when I said the enemy attacked our family for years. What we've been through is no laughing matter. It has hurt and effected each person in various ways, *this* is just *my* story. But you know what? That experience made me strong. Isn't it funny how there are times in our lives where we get no say whatsoever in what happens to us, but then all of a sudden it becomes our responsibility to clean up the mess? Then it's on us to deal with the effects, to learn what to do with the emotional turmoil, trauma, and toxic behaviors that were once the makeup of our entire lives.

Because then you're an adult and it doesn't matter what you're childhood looked like, it's on you to make healthy decisions and not let your anger get the best of you. It can be more than tough sometimes, but you *can't* blame your childhood forever, it's one thing to analyze where your bad habits stem from, and it's another thing to make excuses and blame your past. You have to stop making excuses and take ownership of your life. The great news is that you get to decide what your life looks like and you get to decide what kind of person you want to be. Your past can shape you or it can deteriorate you. The wonderful thing is you get to choose. I chose to take the pain and let it make me stronger, relentless, smarter, and wiser.

I'm not perfect. My past has left me emotionally hurt and I've had to navigate through that. I've had to work hard to not *let* my past trauma consume me and destroy my future. It's not as simple as choosing once, you have to choose every single day. You have to assess your life and realize what negative things you don't want to carry with you into your next season. I failed at this so many times.

Too many times in fact- I've let my emotions get the best of me and hurt people around me. I know I've taken my pain and bled on people who didn't hurt me. I've let my contaminated emotions led me to lash out in anger or bitterness that ended up hurting a lot of good relationships. Don't bleed on people, friends. Though, I understand that it's not always as simple as a choice either. That's the first step, but it doesn't always get you all the way there.

A hard reality I've had to face as a young adult is that I probably need some therapy. When I turned eighteen and went off to do my own thing in life, my past trauma never led me to drug addiction, alcohol abuse, bad decisions, darkness, depression, thoughts of suicide, or any wild thing like that so I figured I was just fine. I assumed that because I didn't have a crazy, irrational ordeal, that the effects of what I went through as a kid "wore off ", or maybe they just didn't affect me as much as I thought. What I quickly learned is that there isn't one way to deal with trauma; the effects look different on everyone. I seemed fine on the outside which led me to believe I was fine. But my toxic traits and mental instability made me second guess.

It stopped me in my tracks. I would get very angry and do things I would come to regret. I would randomly get flashbacks of very specific traumatic events that played over, and over in my mind. It would give me a peculiar reaction, like a bug crawling around in my head; I just wanted to get it out. Eventually, I realized that wasn't normal, or okay even in the slightest bit. I ended up seeing a therapist who told me what I was experiencing was, PTSD, (Post Traumatic Stress Disorder).

Again, I haven't shared all of my story or the specific things that have happened in my life, so trying to explain that I live with/have PTSD to someone who doesn't know the full magnitude of what I've been through feels a bit silly at best. I always thought PTSD was something one who's been to war lives with when they return home. But PTSD is a condition triggered by either experiencing or witnessing a terrifying event. Symptoms include anxiety, flashbacks, nightmares, and uncontrollable thoughts about the event, and it can affect anyone. It does not discriminate. My primary symptom was that last one.

I could be driving, drinking coffee, lying in bed, walking my dog, showering, sitting at my desk, working, and something would trigger me into flashbacks and uncontrollable thoughts. Sometimes I can pray my way out of it, and sometimes it sends me into tears. It's never something I openly spoke about. I kept it to myself because I didn't know what to do with that information. I, like most people, don't like speaking about my past traumas or PTSD. It still feels so weird to call it that. Because even though my conscious mind knows that's not my life anymore, I've gotten through it, everything's alright. My subconscious mind somehow knows that I was seriously hurt and those wounds are still there.

So now and then I'll be reminded that I have past wounds that are still working to become fully healed. So, here's the deal. We have to invest in healing from past trauma. The hardest thing I've had to do in my life is to forgive people who never said sorry for the immense pain and damage they caused me. That is so challenging and debilitating, at times. But it must be done. The healing process is not pretty. But it's so necessary. The reason I share a part of my testimony with you is that I believe if you're going to preach about healing and forgiveness you have to do so from a place of experience.

As I said, the healing process is not pretty, it's hard. It's ugly. Sometimes you *have* to relive some really hard things and it will hurt. You have to go through crucial steps and follow directions to heal effectively. One of the biggest mistakes we make is thinking our physical being is more important to invest in and take care of than our mental being. Health is an all-around thing. If you go to the gym every day and have ripped arms, and are physically healthy- great.

But if your minds not healthy, *you*, as a whole will not be healthy. We want to be healthy, vibrant, and active. We want energy and vitality. But we can never reach full, dynamic health if we continue to put our mental, emotional, and spiritual existence on the back burner. True health is all-around health. Mind, body, and spirit. Therefore, investing in mental health and healing will change your life.

I know that therapy can be expensive and inaccessible for some that's why I didn't go for a while. But there are other ways to work on healing.

HOW WE CAN BEGIN THE HEALING PROCESS:

1. **READ BOOKS**. Books have shaped my mindset so much, it's a huge reason why I'm even writing my own. They have provided me with guidance, knowledge, healing, and steps to take to have emotional vitality. Reading and absorbing knowledge is a huge step in learning how to do anything in life. Execution is the next part

2.   SPEND TIME BY YOURSELF AND WITH GOD. Being alone with God to just pray and give our baggage to him is extremely healing and therapeutic. Knowing that he takes our pain so we don't have to carry it around is remarkable. We just have to be willing to continue laying it at his feet. Reading encouraging scripture, going to church, or just listening to worship music has been my saving grace when it comes to dealing with trauma.

3.   WRITE AN IMPACT LETTER. I heard someone talk about this one day and I just couldn't get it out of my head. So I sat down with a thick notebook and a pen and just wrote everything that's ever happened in my life. I wrote it in detail. I wrote how it affected me, hurt me, and broke my heart. I cried all over that notebook. *But* I felt a little bit of weight come off my back. A weight that I had been hauling around for years. Writing is a powerful thing; sometimes we just need to get our thoughts out on paper before we can rationalize anything. These are just some of the things that have helped me, along with therapy and intentional healing practice. You need to know that your well-being is *worth* fighting for. So get up and fight. Do what it takes to heal, repair, revive, restore and recover your life. You're worth it.

FORGIVNESS AND HEALING

Learning to forgive and let go was a huge part of my healing process. Needless to say, I spent a lot of time angry and upset about my past, as mentioned in the last chapter. My heart was broken. I was hurt. I was upset. I didn't always make great decisions with that pain in my heart. Unfortunately, I let my anger out on a lot of people I cared about, which only hurt me more.

It was this endless cycle of allowing my pain to fester until I got angry and lashed out at people who didn't deserve it which, in the end, just caused more sadness. I needed to learn how to deal with the chaos and heartache of my childhood. But I also needed to forgive; forgiveness isn't just something we say, it is something we act on. Forgiveness is a hard thing to talk about because I feel like some people stand behind it and some people refuse to forgive. It's a hard thing to encourage people to do because part of me feels like, "Who am I to tell someone else how to handle their pain?" For a long time, I thought that forgiveness was something you did once you finally got over that thing that hurt you a long time ago. It meant "getting over it".

When really, forgiveness is a choice not based on feeling. It's a choice you make, most of the time, when you still hurt. Forgiveness is a means to freedom. Forgiveness is a choice, not a feeling. At some point, I had to forgive the people who hurt, or wronged me. I had to forgive and let go of the things I had to go through - the situations I was put in, the things I had to see, the things I had to give up, the person I had to be. Things I never should have had to experience.

I was angry for a long time because of my childhood. I was angry at my parents, I was angry at God, I was angry that nobody helped me when I was scared. I was angry that I had to wait and pray for eleven years before my parents finally stopped fighting and separated. You get the point; I was just plain angry and had to clean up the mess in my

heart, and mind. I was mad at the world, God, and my life. Though I found that it's *okay* to be angry.

But I also found that if you stay that way, it only damages you and harms the people around you. At some point I had to realize that my anger wasn't reconciling any relationships, it wasn't providing me any healing or comfort, it wasn't making the memories go away, it wasn't fixing anything. It was just making *me* miserable. It's okay to be angry about you're past but it's not okay to stay that way.

What I found out was, forgiveness would provide relief from the weight of those things. Not all at once, but with each choice to forgive, a little bit of weight came off of my shoulders-another burden would be released. But it was extremely hard. Anger certainly makes it hard to forgive. Resentment makes it hard to forgive. And forgiving someone and still having resentment in your heart is *not* full forgiveness. One of the hardest parts about forgiving was forgiving people who *never* said sorry.

That's was a tough one. There wasn't an I'm sorry for emotionally and physically abusing you, I'm sorry for the trauma I caused, I'm sorry for putting you in danger, I'm sorry for coming in and wrecking your family, I'm sorry for hurting the people you love in front of you. None of that. But I realized that at the end of the day the people who hurt me don't deserve to have a hold on me anymore, and those who hurt you don't deserve to have a hold on you either. Forgiveness is more about you having *freedom* than it is about *who* hurt you. We are to forgive others just as God has forgiven us. We are supposed to take that same forgiveness that we didn't deserve, turn around and give it to others.

Now, I don't know what you've been through, maybe you've been through worse and don't believe anyone can expect you to forgive. I don't know your pain, but I do want you to know that forgiveness isn't subject to the depth of pain. It is to be done no matter the pain. Some things are much harder to forgive than others, but it provides the same freedom. I'm still forgiving things that happened to me. It's a process. But I believe that forgiveness is critical in *anyone's* journey of healing.

Below is a plethora of *Bible* verses that have resonated with me on my journey to healing- therefore, I hope they resonate with you.

-"For if you forgive other people when they sin against you, your heavenly Father will also forgive you." (*New International Version*-Matthew 6:14)

-"Forgive, and you will be forgiven". (*New International Version*-Luke 6:37)

-"Be kind and compassionate to one another, forgiving each other, just as in Christ God forgave you."(*New International Version*-Ephesians 4:32)

-"So if the Son sets you free, you will be free indeed". (*New International Version*-John 8:36)

-"It is for freedom that Christ has set us free. Stand firm, then, and do not let yourselves be burdened again by a yoke of slavery". (*New International Version*-Galatians 5:1)

-"You, my brothers and sisters, were called to be free. But do not use your freedom to indulge the flesh; rather, serve one another humbly in love". (*New International Version*-Galatians 5:13)

- "Now the Lord is the Spirit, and where the Spirit of the Lord is, there is freedom". (*New International Version*-2 Corinthians 3:17)

Along my journey, I have found that blame will only drag you down in life. It will have control over your actions, it will shape you into the kind of person who makes excuses. There is such power in knowing that you are in control. Regardless of what has happened to you in the past or any circumstance, or right now, at this moment, know that you are in complete control. One of the best things you can do for yourself is to take ownership of where you are at. I believe this is such a hard thing for us, human beings to grasp because we have gotten so accustomed to blaming our circumstances on whoever, or whatever we can.

We use blame as a crutch and if you ever want to have a meaningful life, you won't be able to take that crutch with you. I for one, was guilty of this. I would blame my issues on my tough childhood night and day until I realized that I was the only person solely responsible for the way my life looked. Nobody was holding a gun to my head forcing me to make the decisions I was making. One of the most valuable phrases I adopted was: "It's on me". It is hard to think this way when you've had bad things happen to you. Maybe you have the right to blame someone for how you feel, but it won't get you far.

An important thing to know is that no matter what, you will *never* have the right to blame someone for your reactions. We can't control what happens to us, but we can control how we react to it. Call it manifestation, the law of attraction, vibes, energy, whatever. I honestly believe it's just called *attitude*. There is so much power in our attitudes. When you can take ownership of your life and situations, you get to be in control, that way it's not left up to chance.

FINDING GRATITUDE AND POSITIVITY

Something that will break the chains of negativity in your past, is finding positivity in your past. First comes forgiveness and next comes gratitude- something I'm still working on every day. When I first heard of this gratitude concept I about choked. I thought, how can I possibly be grateful for what happened to me and my family? It was the biggest joke. For a while, I wasn't ready to view my past with a heart, or mind of positivity and gratitude; I was angry, remember? But eventually, I was able to start looking on the bright side and it truly changed my life. Now, I look back on my life and I'm so grateful for so many things.

First, I'm grateful for what God has done in my life and my family. God has...

- Pulled me through and guarded my heart against deep depression and anxiety about my past.
- Brought healing and restoration in my heart and mind.
- Blessed me with a great man who is slow to anger, loves, seeks adventure, pushes me out of my comfort zone, and challenges me to be better
- Protected my siblings and guarded my family.
- Provided me with peace and comfort that surpasses all understanding.

Through it all, there was one thing I went back to time after time after time, heartbreak after heartbreak, loss after loss, the one consistent thing in my life is *who* I ran back to God. I ran to him for everything. I've been a prayer warrior since I was seven – because I had to be. I couldn't do anything but pray. I prayed so much, every day. I learned to pray as my life depended on it because sometimes, I truly thought it did.

And I have so much to be thankful for because God did answer my prayers. He did keep my siblings and me safe. He did keep my parents safe. He did pull us out of toxic and dangerous situations, He did restore relationships; He did bless me with good friends, a community, a church to be a part of, a home, and a close relationship with Him. It's always been Him; by my side, fighting the battles with me. He never left me. Many times, I was tempted to think God wasn't doing anything. I had to keep the faith because I didn't see anything change for a long time.

I had to keep the faith. If you think for one second that God isn't working on your behalf right now as you read these words, you must not know how big our God is. God is faithful, He is always listening, He will never leave you or forsake you. He came to give you life to the fullest; life in abundance. He is the ultimate healer and comforter. He brings peace and restoration. He promises that we won't ever have to fight our battles alone, in fact, He fights our battles *for* us. He works on our behalf. And all you must do is keep your faith in Him. One of my favorite quotes by Joseph Simmons reads, "Stop telling God how big your problem is and start telling your problem how big your God is."

Talk about big faith. I learned to have big faith. So now, when I walk through hardship, rocky waters, sadness, discouragement, setbacks, I have so much faith that God will provide because I know what he has already brought me out of. The number one thing that has gotten me through tough times is looking back and remembering the crazy things God has already revived me from. God has fulfilled all of those promises in my life. The same promises he makes to all of us.

It didn't happen right when I wanted it to, but it happened in His perfect timing. There couldn't be a better time for me to be walking in the fullness of God's glory and provision. Keeping my faith in Him and His promises instead of relying solely on what my life *looked* like was the best decision I've ever made.

GOD IS FAITHFUL:

-"Know therefore that the Lord your God is God; he is the faithful God, keeping his covenant of love to a thousand generations of those who love him and keep his commandments." (*New International Version*-Deuteronomy 7:9)

-"Who is like you, Lord God Almighty? You, Lord, are mighty, and your faithfulness surrounds you." (*New International Version*-Psalm 36:8)

-"If we confess our sins, he is faithful and just and will forgive us our sins and purify us from all unrighteousness." (*New International Version*-1 John 1:9)

Being grateful brings positivity back into the picture. You don't have to necessarily be grateful for your past. I'm sure there are things we would have rather not had to go through. But you can be grateful for where you are and what you have now.

CREATING CLARITY

In the first section of this book, we did some soul searching and decluttered some space to make new. This is the part where we get to lay a solid foundation and start *fresh* with a clean slate. I want to talk about clarity because it's such a fundamentally important step of rising up to new heights in life. If you aim at nothing, you'll hit it every time. You have to have some sort of a target; a goal in mind. I'd say most of us have a dream for our lives.

But as I look around, I see a lot of people who have been practically living their lives for other people way too long, therefore, they have no idea what they even want for *themselves*. Maybe you feel stuck in a job or the mundane day-to-day. The sad truth about devoting your whole life to other people's needs or wants is that your life ends up not truly being *yours*. Even if you're a Mother or Father, or, a caretaker, or teacher - you need to have goals for yourself.

You need to have a vision for where your life is heading. You need a reason to jump out of bed in the mornings because *it is your* life and you have complete permission to fully enjoy it. You have the right to love your life. Not just merely tolerate it. You're not a bystander of your own life so stop spectating and start participating.

Your desires and passions should be a priority because I believe God places dreams in our hearts for a reason. I see it as kind of a road map for what my purpose is. If something is stirring up inside you, an aspiration to achieve something, and you don't go a day without thinking about it, take that as a sign that you should pursue it.

The problem is that a lot of us put our dreams on the backburner for a long time because of two key beliefs:

1. WE DON'T THINK WE HAVE TIME OR ENERGY TO REACH THAT GOAL

2. WE DON'T THINK WE ARE EQUIPPED OR CAPABLE OF REACHING THAT GOAL

I understand that feeling, but until you decide to take your goals seriously, you will go through your life as a *bystander*. Maybe you'll watch other people live out your dreams because you didn't take them seriously enough to have taken any kind of action towards them. We get so caught up in the mundane that we never achieve anything big. Maybe you get inspired for a day or maybe even a week during New Years, but then you slowly fade back into the day-to-day routines and fall back into accommodating everyone else. I have a habit of making my mind up about a goal and throwing myself in without having a clue what I'm doing and just figuring out on the way.

Take, for example, writing a book. I had no idea what I was getting myself into. Not a minute goes by when I think this whole thing is a joke and I should just give up. But I *don't* because I've learned that if I don't make this dream happen, *someone else will*. I've watched people live out my dreams because I was too afraid to do it and, let me tell you, it does not feel good. Somewhere out there someone less talented than you is crushing the thing you dream of doing because they had the pure audacity to get up and make it happen.

If that doesn't get your butt up, and wanting to spring in action, I don't know what will. I am far from the best writer in the world. I feel unequipped to be writing a book. I failed high school English, (well that was because I didn't do my homework and didn't turn things in on time but, that's another story.) The point is, I had a dream to write a book, put my experiences down on paper and share my testimony. I felt in my heart that I have a message to share with people because although I am young, I was forced to grow up fast. I've been through a lot of life and learned a lot of lessons. It would be downright selfish of me to keep my experiences and never share the valuable things I've learned. Will everyone get it or see the value in my message? No. But I don't care. I had a pull on my heart to do this. I felt God leading me to write my story and message and so I took my dream seriously, made it a priority, and rolled with it. I had to stop thinking it needed to be perfect to do it and just do it. I hope you'll take the same approach to that dream of yours that's been tapping you on the shoulder, and whispering into your heart because it's not going anywhere. But one day it will turn from a dream to regret *if* you keep ignoring it. Starting can be the hardest part sometimes, but know that your dreams *are* worthy. They are worth the effort and the prioritization.

You have specific dreams for a reason, don't suppress them. It feels so good to take action on the things your heart has been longing for. Okay, now we know that everyone has dreams for their lives, big or small, and we know the importance of taking action and pursuing them. But what if they're just not that inspiring? Like sometimes it sounds fun to go to cosmetology school and learn hairdressing but other days, you're content with your job at the office. Sometimes you're inspired, sometimes you're not. My thoughts? It could be one of two things. Either you're not dreaming big enough or you're not clear about what you want. Or both. If cosmetology school doesn't light your fire, that's because that's not your end goal.

You have to think beyond that. Think bigger picture. Have an end goal in mind that *does* light your fire. Maybe your end goal is to own your hair salon and become your boss doing something you love every day. *your dreams should scare you a little.* If you know the exact steps to reach your goal right off the bat, you're aiming way too low. Many people don't like the feeling of having big dreams because they can't see all the steps laid out in front of them, (me). But it's not about knowing all the details.

It's about asking yourself what you truly want for your life, why you want it, what it will provide for you/your family and choosing a dream that excites the hell out of you. Something that fuels your fire and keeps you going. Now, with all of this being said, you may be wondering how exactly you can take the steps to build your dreams. Below I have laid out a practical exercise that has aided me in taking the steps toward not only building my dreams but also bringing them to fruition.

HOW WE CAN BUILD OUR DREAMS: If you feel stuck and have no idea what you want for your life, BUT you do know you want to achieve better and greater, do this dream building exercise.

1. **WHAT IS YOUR ULTIMATE VISION FOR YOUR LIFE?** Don't think, just write. Write everything that makes you think of a happy, full, content, fun, adventurous, abundant life. What are your biggest dreams and goals? Set a timer for 5 minutes and just write everything that comes to mind.

2. **OUT OF THAT LIST CHOOSE YOUR TOP 1-3 DREAMS/GOALS:** What are the top one to two dreams that feel the MOST valuable to you? Which top goals hold the most meaning to you or have the biggest impact on you and those around you?

3. **WHAT IS YOUR WHY FOR EACH OF THESE GOALS/DREAMS?** This is extremely important to figure out because without a why there is no purpose and you won't follow-through. Your why can be anything. As long as it's meaningful to you and drives you. Your why should be the thing that keeps you driven and motivated to follow through with your goal. It's the reason it's necessary to accomplish your goal.

4. **WHAT WILL THIS PROVIDE FOR YOU?**
   You have to know how accomplishing this goal/dream will positively affect your life.

5. **HOW WILL THIS IMPACT OTHERS?**

   This can be the biggest driving force behind doing what you do, simply because we feel called to do things for other people; we want to leave a positive impact on people, to serve and better their lives. This exercise always helps me feel more clarity and sincerity about my goals/ dreams because I *challenge* myself to see the importance of it.

Now you have your 'why'; the driving force behind *why you do what you do*. This exercise helps to narrow down a couple of goals that you should be focusing on. It helps if you feel jumbled up and overwhelmed with a plethora of ideas, and it also helps if you feel stuck and have no idea where to begin or what to pursue. Regardless of where you're at, this exercise provides *clarity* which is a necessity when it comes to goalsetting. Next, I want you to make a vision board. Yes, just like in fifth grade.

Whip out the poster board, gel pens, sharpies, glue sticks, print some pictures, cut out some magazine words, gather some inspirational quotes and go for it. This is fun and crafty, but its ultimately about putting all your passions and dreams and goals in one place. Its purpose is to remind you every day what you're working for. When we don't know what we're working for, we get stuck in the day-to-day mundane. You need to know that there's more. A vision board serves to fuel you up; and inspire you to keep going.

It reminds me that I'm going to do big things and eventually, I

started reaching those goals I had been writing down for months. It makes me excited and fired up. So do it. Write down your dreams of going on a Hawaiian vacation, paying down your student loan debt, getting a dog, starting a business, becoming a first-generation millionaire, going back to school, making a passive income, writing a book, etc., Write it down every day, it will take two minutes. And watch how it transforms your life.

This dream building exercise will give you more clarity, and direction to take your ambition. But what if you know what you want? What if your problem is that you want so many things and you don't know what to focus on, you try to do everything and in result, nothing gets achieved. This is me, all the way. A multi-passionate creative entrepreneur, if you will. I have a lot of hobbies and things I enjoy doing. It's hard to choose one thing because I just want to accomplish all of my goals at once. I had my hands in lots of baskets because there were so many things that sounded fun and exciting to me. The problem was, I wasn't getting anywhere with my goals.

Sure, I was doing a lot and felt "busy" but I couldn't get any of my dreams to take off because I was trying to focus on way too many. I used to think that I should only want to accomplish one big thing. Maybe two. But there *isn't* anything wrong with having multiple ambitions. However, we can't do ten different things at once and do them all well. If you want to get good at something, it's going to take all of your focus, time, and energy.

I was trying to divide all my attention between several goals; building my photography business, writing my book, saving for real-estate investments, and learning how to do it, building my network marketing business, attending all the business training events, going to the gym, pursuing health and wellness, taking on a wedding photography internship, going to my *Bible* study on Tuesdays, serving at church on Sundays, yoga on Thursdays and Fridays, on top of my forty-hour a week job.

Not to mention the adult responsibilities like grocery shopping, checking the oil, doing the dishes, laundry... You know, all that stuff (thank you to sweet baby Jesus that I don't have children). Each of these passions serves as a purpose to help me get to the best version of myself. Healthy and fit, being a successful business owner, building passive income, having involvement with my church and my friend group, strong faith. But all it was doing, ultimately, was causing me to burn out.

I couldn't possibly devote the time it took to be good at *all* these things. And because I never made real progress in anything I did, I felt discouraged and like I just wasn't good enough. I had heard about the importance of choosing one goal at a time to work on, but I kind of brushed it off and stuck to what I wanted to do: everything. The more I took on and got involved in, the more things were constantly pulling at my attention, time, and energy. I was so burnt out. I remember driving to my internship meeting and freaking out because I had so much going on that I wasn't even looking forward to learning or being present in this opportunity, instead I was thinking about everything else that needed to get done instead.

When you don't narrow down your priorities, you're just running around doing mindless tasks that are *supposed* to be fun but in reality, are just draining. My problem was that I didn't want to choose *one thing*. I didn't know how I'd choose just one thing when I had so many goals and visions for my life. For a long time, I refused, but I hit a wall. Once I finally sat down and decided I couldn't keep up with everything anymore, things changed. I sat at my desk one night and wrote down all my dreams for the next five-ten years.

I did some reflection on my goals. I asked myself questions like: "How will this dream positively impact my life?" "How will this help other people?", "How will this glorify God and lead people to Him?", "How meaningful, intentional, and purposeful is this goal?". I did this and I immediately knew my answer. The one thing I chose to spend my time and energy focusing on was writing *this* book.

I made it priority number three (after my health and God.) So, it was at the top. From that point on I canceled all other plans. I took time off from my internship, put my business on hold, cleared my schedule so I could spend time writing. I knew this book was the most important goal to achieve for me. There is power in sharing our testimony and I just felt God tell me that this was important and needed to get done first. Great achievements take great focus and attention. I'm telling you, my results skyrocketed. I have the time and energy it takes to do exceptional work.

When you have your hands in too many baskets, you can't do exceptional work in any of those endeavors. I didn't believe it at first either but the truth is, you won't reach full achievement in your goals in any capacity if you don't *make* it your one mission. Working on five different goals at once is like having one body part dipped in five different swimming pools at the same time and calling that "swimming." That's not swimming.

If you want to swim, you've got to pick one pool and jump in. Pick one and go all in. Having parts of you just dipped in things you like only hinders your success and makes everything you do mediocre.

 Pick one and go all in – become great at one thing and then move on to the next goal. Finally choosing one goal instead of seven is the reason you're reading this book right now. If I had chosen to just stick with trying to make everything work at once like a crazy person, I would have gotten burnt out and tossed this book, this goal in the garbage.

Because that's what burn out does. It strips us of our inspiration, deprives us of rest, and it declines our progress rapidly. If you just make a decision, choose to focus on one thing, I promise your results will catapult. The last thing I'll say about this is that when you know your dream, the next step is to give it to God. Here's what I believe; I believe that God has a plan and a purpose for all of our lives. I believe that he has placed dreams and visions within each of us that corresponds with the purpose He's given us.

And I believe that he comes alongside us to co-create and unravel our dreams for His glory. If there is a longing in your heart of something you want to achieve or a dream, I believe it's there because God put it there; there is purpose in your dreams. But it's up to us to take action on it. We have to take a step out in faith when it comes to our goals and make the first move. God placed a dream in your heart, you realize it, you acknowledge it, you take action, and then you give it to God and allow Him to guide you through the steps and allow him to lead you through what it's going to take to reach your goal. After all, if God's the one who put that dream in your heart, who better would know how to accomplish it than

Him? Giving God our dreams allows Him to step in and create ways that otherwise wouldn't be there.

I don't think I could be writing this book right now if it weren't for his provision and guidance. He is leading me on what to say and how to say it and I love it. It's so much better cultivating alongside the ultimate creator instead of trying to figure it all out on my own. Take your dreams to God in prayer every day and watch him intervene, create ways or maybe even steer you to something bigger and better!

REFINING YOUR HABITS

Our habits make up so much of our lives. The point of setting habits is to intentionally lay out what you're choosing to be consistent every day. A habit is something you do consistently. Consciously or unconsciously. The great news is we have the power to choose our habits. A lot of that begins with assessing our current habits and figuring out the bad ones we don't want to keep. For me, that was eating too much candy (hello Sour Patch Kids), drinking too much soda, eating out too much, going way too long without water, and not getting enough sleep. I have a very fast metabolism and like to stay active, so for a while, I didn't see any physical effects of unhealthy eating choices, but I *knew* they were unhealthy.

Sometimes we have to take a step back and realize when there's an unhealthy habit. Even if we don't *see* any negative impacts- we need to make a change. As I said, anything done consistently over time will provide the results in correspondence with that habit. You might not notice anything negative yet, but everything we do compounds and it all affects us sooner or later. If you don't notice any effects of your unhealthy habits, all that means is that the aftermath and the consequences of your unhealthy choices are quickly on their way and this might be your last chance to step in, and stop yourself in your tracks and make a change for the better.

Refining your habits is the process of going through and getting rid of the old while establishing the new. Out with the old, in with the new. But how do we break or create a habit? Through consistency. See? We're getting somewhere! Okay now, it takes twenty-one days to create a habit and ninety days to create a lifestyle. What I recommend is picking one habit to get rid of and only choosing a couple at a time to weave into your daily life.

A mistake I made a few times was trying to get rid of ten habits at once while trying to establish ten new habits. It won't work that way
because habits are something that takes time and diligence to establish or get rid of. Juggling too many at once will just be counterproductive. What I like to do is pick one habit to establish and use the old school tally mark strategy. I put a tally for every day that I've done the habit until I've reached thirty. This means that I'm constantly working on a new habit each month. Maybe you already have some habits in mind that you want to work on, but I want to list a few things that have fundamentally changed my life after doing daily-

PRAYER

Taking a few minutes to pray every day has shifted my mind and heart so much. It gives me a sense of peace and knowing that God is alongside me helping me, crying with me, celebrating with me, encouraging me, and comforting me. The wonderful part about it is that it doesn't have to be in a church, it doesn't have to be anywhere special and there's no right or wrong way to do it. It's just *talking* to God. I like to pray in my car on the way to work but I find myself constantly talking to God throughout the day. I start by thanking him for the day; that I'm alive and healthy and walking and breathing through another day. I thank him for my job, my home, my relationship, and the car I'm driving.

I invite Him into the day with me, so that I would feel His presence throughout the day, His peace comfort, and joy; I then pray for the people I love, that He would keep them safe and healthy and happy. I give Him my dreams *every day*. Lately, I've been specifically praying over this book. I've been praying that He would come alongside me and create this book with me, that He would give me the right words to spill onto the pages, and that it would be a reflection of His character.

That's it.

Every day I do that. This is just my example but your prayer is specific to you and your relationship with God, it doesn't need to be fancy

or rehearsed or staged. But talking to God daily about what's on your heart will produce a shift in your life and your mind. After doing this for a while I notice more peace in my life. I noticed a weight that came off of my shoulders because I know that I'm not here to do life alone, I know that God is always with me and always listening to me.

He hears more than I can speak, He hears my heart and all I have to do is invite him into my space and He is there listening and moving on my behalf. So pray. Pray in the shower, at your desk, in your car, in the mountains, at church, at work, at home, at the airport. It doesn't matter where you do it, it just matters that you do it because making a habit out of praying daily will fundamentally change your life.

EXERCISE

I grew up as an athlete, so exercise has always been an important part of my life. Working out is something that increases my health, but it also increases my vitality, energy, and focus each day. It has become so incredibly important to me. Exercise releases endorphins, which make you happy. Getting in a 30-minute sweat session each day will boost your mood substantially. The great news about exercise is that you can modify it to fit your needs. There are so many great options out there.

Yoga, Pilates, CrossFit, running, weight lifting, Zumba, walking your dog to the park, dancing, sports. You don't need a gym membership to start pursuing exercise. I promise you can go on a walk around your neighborhood each day. I get the same effect after a nice long walk as I do after an intense lifting session at the gym. Get out every day and sweat a little.

The way I see it, we have twenty-four hours in a day and spending one of those hours doing something hard like working out has the power to positively affect the other twenty-three. It energizes you, clears your mind, and even helps you sleep better! Prioritize one hour a day for exercise and see the benefits for yourself.

WRITING

I have been writing things down since the womb, as I like to say. I love lists and charts and journals and notes and I spend way too much money in the notebook aisle at Target. Writing every day is a way for me to get my thoughts out and on paper. It's a way for me to organize my ideas and strategize how I want to achieve certain goals. What has shifted my life is writing down gratitude and affirmations daily. This is a form of mindset training, as it shapes the way you think and brings positivity into the picture.

When you list five things your grateful for every day, it sets you up to constantly be looking around you for things to be *grateful* for. That's a huge and significant mindset shift that is *important* for rising up. Getting in the habit of writing down gratitude's, affirmations, and goals every day will leave significant impacts on your life. Along with the tally mark strategy, there is another way I love to track my habits.

I take a piece of graph paper and each block represents one day. I make a box with seven rows across for each day of the week. On the right side, I write down one habit on each row. Things like the gym, writing gratitude and affirmations, meditating, drinking enough water. I limit it to about five until I feel like I've really got the hang of one habit, and then I swap it out for another. So, my habit tracker looks something like a graph chart and each day I color in the box after I have done a certain habit.

This is not necessary, but it does offer a visual representation of your consistency. Another option would just be using your planner or a calendar and each day coloring in a circle representing the completion of the habit you're trying to establish. Anything that allows you to see your patterns visually and track your consistency will help you see how you're doing and where any holes are. Maybe you'll notice that you don't keep up with your habits as much on weekends or after long days in the week.

It will allow you to assess and readjust to get those habits in. It will also help you keep track of how long you've been doing that habit. The point of diligently working on establishing a habit is so that one day, it becomes second nature to you. It's tough to establish a new habit because you *do* have to think about it every day. You have to set reminders on your phone, write it in your planner, sometimes I even have to get out of bed after just getting in because I forgot to finish my last bit of water for the day.

It's not easy, it's tedious and annoying but one day you'll start doing it without even thinking about it. That's the money. That's the goal here and what we're after. It's not about doing tiny, tedious things that have minimal significance, it's about establishing things that will impact us positively long term, *not* short term. The truth is, drinking half your body weight in water every day doesn't seem like much for one day. It just makes you have to pee a lot.

But the impact that has over a week? Two weeks? A month? You'll feel more awake, clear-headed, hydrated, and alert. The thing about habits is that you *won't* notice a change right away and that can lead you to just stop altogether. But you have to remember the long term effects when establishing a new habit. Have a great why and remember *how* this will make your life better in the long term. It's about creating a new lifestyle for yourself. A better lifestyle. That's all we're doing here when working on our habits.

Little by little, one small decision after another, creating the life you want for yourself. If you want to be a writer one day, get in the habit of writing a page in a journal every day. If you want to be a runner, get in the habit of getting outside every day to run. If you want better health, cut out some junk food. If you want more energy, start drinking two bottles of water a day. Every goal you have for yourself and your life starts with one tiny decision that you make right now.

Do something that will lead you to your goal right now. And then do that same thing tomorrow. And again the next day. And again the next day. And the next. And the next. And the next. Keep pushing, track your progress, set reminders on your phone, put sticky notes on your mirror, and do it every day no matter what. And soon you won't need the reminders or the sticky notes or the habit tracker, because it will be second nature to you.

You won't even have to think about it anymore, you'll just do it because now, that's who you are. Who you become in the next few months is completely contingent on the decisions you make and the things you start doing *right now*. It may take a while to see your ultimate vision for your goal, but it doesn't take long to start seeing some results, some changes, some shifts in your mind, body, attitude, emotions, health, etc...

All it takes is one positive thing that you do every day without fail, no matter what.

THE VALUE OF CONSISTENCY

What you do everyday matters. Your habits matter. And the way we establish great habits is through consistency. Consistency is the difference between achieving a big goal and having a hobby. Almost nothing will take off without diligent, consistent action. Consistency is one of the most important things to get good at because it's the dictating factor in your results. If your consistently underperforming, cutting corners, quitting; if you're consistently lazy, uninspired, unmotivated, you will get results according to those actions.

Good or bad, you get the results of whatever you do consistently. Not once or twice, but over and over and over again. That's why whenever I set a new goal for my fitness and I am tempted to get discouraged when I look in the mirror and don't see any change, I tell myself this, "You don't get to complain about your results. You don't get to be upset about you're lack of results when you haven't done the work to get them. You can assess yourself after you've followed through and done the consistent work necessary."

That way of thinking brings logic back into the picture. How can we expect to see results or change when we haven't done any hard work consistently for more than a week at most? You cant. There's nothing to base your analysis off when there's not hours and hours and hours of work put into your craft. You don't go swimming once and then become an Olympic swimmer. You don't start up a business one day and make a thousand dollars the next day.

You don't write one page and become an author. You don't quit your addiction for one night and stop being an addict. You don't go to the gym once and get abs. You don't eat one salad and get skinny. You don't walk your dog once and he's good to go for life. You don't wake up early one day and all of a sudden it's easy and natural. You don't write your goal down one morning and by that afternoon, it's a dream come true. I hope you get the point. Success *doesn't* happen by something we do one time.

Even if that one thing is a big jump. Like signing up for a gym membership, getting rid of all the candy in the house, buying a new book to read or a new planner. All things I've done. They're big steps in the right direction. But even big steps don't do the trick. It won't give you lasting results. Sustainable success only comes from doing something over and over and over and over. Every single day. *Not* just once in a while. Babe Ruth said this, "Today's home runs don't win tomorrow's games". Isn't that the truth?

It doesn't matter what moves you make today if you're not consistent with them every day. I have goals to get fit and healthy but at some point, I had to tell myself that if I was only going to go to the gym once in a while, here and there, eat like trash and not give it my all, I should just stop going altogether. That's a waste of a $20 gym membership. I had to tell myself that if I wasn't going to use my planners and goal sheets and gratitude journals every damn day and fill those pages, I needed to just stop buying them. Because doing something here and there just shows that it's not that important and it's more of a hobby. That's completely understandable behavior towards something that is your hobby, but for something that is a serious goal for your life, that lack-luster performance will never cut it.

You'll be running around in the same circle for years with no change if you don't decide right now to start doing things that *matter* consistently. Consistency is what produces the results you want. Small, precise tasks that don't seem like much will compound and add up. Again, whether that's good or bad. You need to develop consistency for each of your goals. So, how do you develop consistency? *Develop commitment.* When you're committed to your goal, you work on it every single day until it's complete.

If you find yourself having a consistency problem, ask yourself, "Do I have a commitment issue?". When you're committed, you show up every day whether you want to or not. My parents did a great job teaching me commitment. When I joined the basketball team as a freshman, I quickly realized that I hated playing competitive basketball. I'm not physically aggressive, I don't enjoy being touched or having people up in my space, I didn't understand it.

I was there to have fun and learn basketball and of course win games. But the girls I played with had been playing basketball their whole lives, basketball was their life. It was not my life. I didn't enjoy the tough nature of the game because I wasn't passionate about it. I didn't want to follow through with it. But I decided to be on the team and my parents told me that I needed to honor my commitment to the team and follow-through. That taught me a lot.

When you commit to someone or something, you need to follow through and fulfill that commitment. But the same thing can be said about you. When you commit yourself, you *need* to honor it. The more time you brush off a commitment or you don't show up ready for it every day, little by little you become a person who doesn't keep promises to yourself. And that becomes a habit. Do not underestimate the ugly habit that can be created by continually blowing off commitments. You'll soon discover that you can't keep commitments to anything, even yourself, the more you blow them off. It does not feel good.

As time goes by you will wonder why nothing sticks, why you start something exciting but can never seem to finish it, and it's because you've formed a habit of not pursing your commitments consistently. Get in a serious habit of taking your commitments seriously and executing them consistently. Consistency can be hard to achieve when you have too many commitments lined up.

But as we've talked about before, narrow down your commitments, don't be afraid to say no, get clear about what you want, analyze the actions/steps it will take to reach your goal, and execute. Execution should be your favorite word. We live in one of the most over-knowledge under- executed societies. We love to learn and plan and research but when it comes time to do the work, we would rather just do more learning, planning, and researching. which will not work at all. Ever. I've had to learn this for myself, the real magic is *in* the execution, *not* the planning.

So set yourself up for success by doing what most people will not do. Make the hard decisions every day that will take you in the direction of your goals/dreams.

SELF-DISCIPLINE

Habits shape who we are, which are developed through consistency, which is developed through discipline. I love talking about self-discipline because it's hard and uncomfortable, it takes grit and resilience. It's one of the most valuable skills you can ever have. The ability to get yourself to do hard things with nobody else there to make you or hold you accountable is how we truly rise up. If you base your productivity on your feelings, you will stay in the same spot for the rest of your life.

Anything worth having takes discipline and if you're an adult, there will not always be someone by your side holding your hand making sure you do what you said you would do. I love a good old accountability partner. I love having a coach. It's great. But it's the days that I have to wake up on my own at 4:50 a.m. to brush snow off my car and drive myself to the gym with nobody else around to "suffer with me" that has built my character. The things you are disciplined about shape your character and propel you to the next level and the truth is that on your journey towards hitting your goal, you *will* have hard days.

You will have to do hard things and you will be challenged greatly. You won't feel like working, that's a certainty. But you can't afford to let your feelings dictate your decisions. Feelings are fickle and unreliable to a great extent. When you know what your goal is, you've assessed the actions towards getting to that goal, you have to do the work. Knowledge with no action is useless. Action makes it happen.

There is no way, that I know of, to teach self-discipline. It can only be developed. When I decided to do high-school online instead of going to a public school, something shifted. It was now on me to make sure everything got done that was required on my end to graduate. It was all on me. I loved it and I hated it.

I believe we like to be in control, but when it's time to do the work and nobody is around us to cheer us on, coach us, or motivate us, suddenly we don't want that dream, or goal as much. There were many, many times I wanted to quit high-school. But It was the discipline that got me through school. It was the discipline that made me a first place soloist at fifteen in my very first dance competition. It was the discipline that led me to get this far in writing this book.

Discipline is how things get done. If you can't be disciplined you won't reach your goal. So, you may be wondering how exactly one can develop self-discipline. Below are ways that have I believe are integral in developing self-discipline.

1. KNOW YOUR WHY AND REMEMBER IT *WHEN* THINGS GET TOUGH

If you don't have a strong why for what you're doing, there's no way you're going to force yourself to do any kind of tough work. You have to have a why and you have to remember it every time you're faced with the choice of getting up, and taking action, or staying in bed and taking a nap. What is the driving force behind why you do what you do? What is the purpose? When you have a strong why and a strong purpose for accomplishing a certain goal, it becomes necessary to discipline your way to meaningful action. If you only ever do what is easy, you will stay stuck and your life will be difficult. But if you do what is difficult at the moment, your life will become easier.

2. REWARD YOURSELF FOR FOLLOWING THROUGH

I know that self-discipline *is* hard. But it doesn't have to be the most miserable thing. One of the best ways to encourage you to take action even when it's the last thing you feel like doing is having something awesome to look forward to. For me, I love chicken wings with a passion. I could eat them every meal every day. I LOVE them. They aren't healthy for you so I've had to cut back quite a bit. But the cool thing is, is that I can treat myself to some buffalo wings after hitting a goal of mine, like going to the gym five days in a row, or hitting my page count for a whole week.

You can even set shorter-term rewards for yourself such as, after waking up an hour early tomorrow to get some extra work done, reward yourself with an iced coffee. Your rewards shouldn't counteract with your goals. Meaning if your goal is to get in shape, I wouldn't suggest having a reward like a cheeseburger for going to the gym. Have small rewards for the little decisions to be disciplined and have bigger rewards for finally hitting a goal.

3. ELIMINATE DISTRACTIONS

When you have endless distractions at your fingertips, you'll always find yourself choosing something over your priority task. When you need time to focus, eliminate as many distractions as possible. Put your phone on silent, turn off the TV, close your door, put your head down and do the work. As long as you have distractions around you, you're only giving your goal half your focus and energy. High achievers don't get to success by multi-tasking. You have to be able to eliminate distractions for one or two solid hours a day to get the most value and productivity out of your work.

4. COUNT TO THREE AND GO

When you know you need to get up and do something but don't feel like it, count one, two, three and force yourself up and in action. This strategy works because it doesn't allow you time to talk yourself out of your task. When you lay around waiting for motivation, it allows you tons of time to overthink and find a way out of it. Count to three, and force yourself to get up and walk yourself out of the room or to your desk or to the car or wherever and *get* to work.

5. REMOVE YOURSELF FROM YOUR ENVIRONMENT

Remove yourself from whatever environment you're in that has you feeling so unmotivated. Maybe that's your Livingroom on the comfy couch and you need to get up and go on a walk in the fresh air. Maybe it's in your bed and you need to go do a few jumping jacks. Whatever place you're in that has you so unmotivated will most-likely keep you in that same state of mind. Something as simple as some sunlight and cool air, or a hot shower, or a drive to a coffee shop, or a freshly clean room, or a walk to the park can trigger your mind to think more positively about your situation.

I thrive so much off of my surroundings. I focus best when I have a clean, light space. So when I have a project I need to focus on for a few hours, I always try and take a few minutes to set up my workspace that will allow me to feel comfortable, organized, awake, and distraction-free. Figure out what your ideal work environment is and do some preparation before sitting down to work. Your workspace can be anything or anywhere you want it to be. But it must be distraction-free if you want to get quality work done in the time you've set aside for it.

6. RESPECT YOURSELF AND YOUR TIME

If you have made it a point to carve out some time to work on your goal, don't waste that time. Get the most value out of that time as you possibly can. You wouldn't schedule a meeting with someone you respect and waste their time, would you? You wouldn't check your phone every 5 minutes, scroll through Instagram, take a cat nap, grab a snack, right? So why would it be okay to waste your own time? It's not. Have respect for yourself and your time, take your goals seriously, just like you would for your boss or your mentor.

7. JUST DO THE DAMN THING

Do what you need to do to get it done. Turn on some gangster rap, drink a cold brew, have a dance party, whatever. But just get to work. Self-discipline is a valuable skill. It's not one that many people have. Sharpening this alone will put you miles ahead of the people who choose comfort over challenge daily. Don't choose comfort because everything your dreaming of for your life is on the other side of an uncomfortable change. Get clear about your goals, figure out what it will take to reach those goals, establish great habits, be consistent, and when it gets hard or uncomfortable, be disciplined. That is how you rise up.

OBTAINING A GROWTH MINDSET

Fixed mindsets are fear-based mindsets. What do I mean by this? This world is filled to the brim with opportunity. Most of us never indulge in possibilities because of our fixed mindsets. Most of us would rather have safety than risk and adventure. To keep our minds fixed on one certain way of doing things or living is to live in fear. To never step out and be open to new things and be adaptive to the changing world is having a fear-based mindset.

We get very comfortable in what's familiar and it becomes scary to ever try to do anything outside of our comfort zones. What I want to share with you in this chapter is how imperative it is to not stay stuck in the same thinking patterns your whole life. The world around you changes. Your life changes. You change. So why should your way of thinking stay the same? We need to work on our adaptability, because when your mindset stays in the same place forever, never growing or adapting, *you* stay in the same place.

You can't accomplish anything with a fixed mindset because what got you here, most of the time, won't get you there. What I mean by that is, the skills, knowledge, and actions that got you to this current place in your life won't be the same skills, knowledge, and actions that get you to an even better place. It will take new thoughts, bigger thinking, broader knowledge, better skillsets. If you fail to refine those things, you will always have a really hard time reaching goals.

Choosing to have a growth mindset instead of a fixed mindset is a requirement. You have to be open to the idea of things changing, open to the idea of trying new things if you're ever going to accomplish your goals. A fixed mindset is set on its ways, uninterested in change or doing things new. It's a very limiting way of thinking because in a world full of people who want to accomplish big and obtain success sure has a lot of people unwilling to do things differently than the way they've always been done. A fixed mindset is a set of chains that have you by the arms holding you to the ways that maybe once worked for you, but the thing is, what worked for you before won't work for you now.

What got you to this level won't be what gets you to the next. One of the biggest examples of a fixed mindset are schools still making it a requirement for kids to apply for colleges and parents pushing kids into going back to school. That is a major fixed mindset because it's taking something that worked for *some* people, and making it something that *everyone* should do. It's a cookie-cutter way of living and as long as that is the standard, sustainable long term success won't have any room to squeeze in. Having a growth mindset is all about adapting and changing and trying new things to get to the next level. It's about refusing to settle, looking for new opportunities, keeping an open mind about what might help you achieve what you want to achieve, and not limiting yourself to doing what everyone and their mother is doing. It's about finding what is going to work and what isn't.

Keep an open mind about things because when you close yourself off to too much and go with the cookie-cutter option, you are forfeiting opportunities that were made to help you launch that dream of yours. Be careful and mindful of your decisions. When you make decisions based on what everyone else is doing or what everyone says you should be doing, that's a fixed mindset. Choosing to stick with what's always worked for you instead of stepping out in faith and taking a risk is a fixed mindset. That mindset will only ever keep you on the level you're at now. But until you develop a growth mindset, you'll stay at that level.

What worked before won't work now. Have the courage to step out in faith in your goals, see what's possible, take risks, don't settle. Stay away from cookie-cutter standards for living, don't keep yourself in a box. If you don't like where you're at, start taking the steps to get where you *want* to be. Be open-minded and open to the idea that maybe you don't know everything. Embrace different options for education, making money, building a career, living.

There are so many amazing platforms out there and it's hard for me to watch young adults struggle and dread their way through college thinking it's the only way because that's what they were told. Step out, explore a new way, or create a new way. But stop keeping yourself in a fixed mentality- embrace the possibility that there *is* more for you than what you've always had or what you've been told you *can* have. There is so much more out there but you'll never experience it from the box you keep yourself in called your fixed mindset.

When I see people either in a work environment or other environments that have extremely fixed mindsets, it makes sense why they've been in the same situation for as long as they have. People with fixed mindsets want everything done a certain way and they want everyone to comply with those standards as well, because not only do they think it's the best and only way, they think everyone should perform that way. This is something to be avoided because like I mentioned, fixed mindsets equal unmoving lives. I urge you to practice

127

stepping outside of the comfort of your structured, safe box and seeing what is possible. Allowing yourself to live life with a growth mindset will open so many more doors for you. We were never made to know it all.

I believe that we were created to collaborate with others, to allow our thinking to be refined and strengthened by the knowledge of other people. Embrace new ideas and new ways to approach your goals throughout your life.

PART THREE:
NEVER SETTLE

THE IMPORTANCE OF ALWAYS WORKING TOWARD BETTER

We have all been guilty of settling for much less than what we deserve. Instant gratification has turned us into people who will settle for whatever we can get as long as we can get it fast. Fast results have become more meaningful to us than quality results. Even if what we've got now is amazing, settling closes off doors to even better things. So many people have settled for good that they have no idea the greatness that exists. There is always more out there.

There is always better, and it's worth fighting for. It's worth not settling for less when you are worthy of so much more in your life. The sad part is, many people will settle for less because it's more comfortable than reaching for something bigger. We live in the land of opportunity, there is no shortage of opportunity out there.

Yet, it amazes me how many people continue to settle with whatever they can get or settle with whatever people tell them is achievable. We are taught, first thing, as adults that we are to settle with whatever we can get. We are not to go and try to achieve things too big or too out there. Our beliefs are squashed as soon as we step foot into adulthood, if not before then. So I talk to people my age in college or out of college that are just utterly dissatisfied with what their degree got them. I talk to kids getting ready to go to college and I see the dread in their eyes.

I ask if they're excited and they reply, "It's not really what I want to do but it will pay well". I believe that's the reason a lot of people go to school. We all want a good job that pays us well. Sure, it would be nice to love what we do but we usually settle for whatever we can get. I wish more eighteen year old's knew how much money they'd be spending to go learn about something they don't want to learn about to get a job they don't want to work, to make money that doesn't allow them *any* freedom.

The thing is, I know plenty of people who go to college and become successful. What's unfortunate is that we are taught from a young age to settle and just do what everyone else is doing, and has been doing for hundreds of years. It sticks in our brains as we get older that we are supposed to keep a closed mind and just stick to what we know or what we have been told is best. We are supposed to keep our heads down and keep our minds fixated. But what good has that done anyone? Sure, maybe it's kept you safe. But it's also kept you from greatness. It's kept you from achieving at the levels you want to be.

It's kept you from freedom and fulfillment in your life. Weighing the options, what would you say is better? I am all for having realistic and achievable goals, but I implore you to be mindful of when you may be aiming too low or settling for less. I have gone through a lot of jobs. Some people called me a "job hopper" because as soon as I got one, I got a different one for about a year. Some may say that's being picky, but I call it not settling. I refuse to settle for less than what I believe I deserve. I could have stuck with whatever job I could get.

Believe me, it was tough getting trained up, learning the companies, finally getting the swing of things and feeling like God was leading me to a different opportunity. It was confusing and tough because I knew it looked like I was just bouncing from job to job and wasn't grateful for what I had. I could have chosen to just stick with what I had learned in my job(s), even though it wasn't the most fulfilling or the best place for me personally. I was comfortable with my job(s). I knew them well, I could answer questions, I knew the companies through and through. But something was off.

It was unfulfilling, unsustainable, and draining. So I would seek out another opportunity and get the same results; I'm excited at first, I go through training, gain all the knowledge, and learn how to do my job well and that voice creeps in again, "This isn't where you're supposed to be". So I quit and find another job. And another. And another.

Call me crazy, but my unwillingness to settle doubled my income within just one year of keeping an open mind to the opportunities that were out there. There is a time to stay and a time to go. Don't be afraid to go just because you're comfortable where you're at. Don't let your comfort steal what could be magnificent and give you the things you've been praying for.

Sometimes we pray for things like a new house, a better job, a better income, a better community, better friends, but when God opens the door and tells us to go, we don't want to. Instead, we want to stay where it's warm and safe and comfortable. And believe me when I say that there is, most definitely, a time to stay and to go. I believe that that's between you and God. Maybe you are called to be in a certain place for a season of your life but when you keep praying, doors keep opening, and you keep staying...

Come on. That is settling. That is playing it safe, and I know how scary it can be to go for it and put yourself out there because anything we do to put ourselves out there is risking judgment. But to not risk is to settle. You can decide which is worse. Playing safe doesn't even guarantee your safety from judgment, so you might as well go all in. It's scary at first, but it feels good not to settle. It feels so good not to settle and to not allow fear to have the last word.

But if I'm being honest with you, what you crave in your life will *require* discomfort. It *will* require you to step into unknown territory and trust God. Embrace discomfort and be open to opportunity, not closed off to it.

IMPROVING YOUR LANGUAGE

This can be applied in so many different situations. How you talk to yourself, how you speak to other people, how you talk about your vision, how you talk about others, how you stand up for yourself. But it can all be summed up by these two words – intentional speaking. How intentional are you in the way you talk? Do you possess a strong, assertive kind, and honoring language? Or do you gossip, curse, bash others, tear yourself down, argue, and insult? You don't have to answer that, but I hope that after this you'll understand that the first set of examples is a requirement.

Speak life into your goals, speak love to others. How you speak matters. If you ever want to be a person of influence, if you ever want to be in a place of leadership, you *need* to speak well. Your language *needs* to be a reflection of your character. Maybe you need to bite your tongue more. Or maybe you need to practice being more direct with people. Either way, you have to speak with intentionality.

The only thing a prideful, stuck up, rude, insulting way of speaking will do, is turn people away. Practice kindness and humility. You can be both assertive and kind. You can be direct and compassionate. You can express yourself without bashing others. You *can* have an issue with someone and not go around gossiping about them.

Leaders are mindful of how they talk. You can't just go around saying anything you feel like. Have self-control about the things you say, speak with intention, and become mindful about the language you use. Immature speaking is a major telling sign of an immature character. How you speak to others is important, but how you talk to yourself is just *as* important. Be aware of how you talk about yourself.

Do you constantly belittle yourself, talk yourself down, criticize your ambitions, or claim yourself unworthy or incapable? How you talk to yourself has such an incredible impact on what kind of result you get in life. How you speak about your dreams impacts whether you pursue them or let them fall to the side. What you say rapidly manifests your reality.

Be mindful of the way you talk about yourself and your actions. Speak life into your goals and ambitions, speak life into others. Become someone who believes great things are always on their way. The simplest way to do this is through affirmations. When you sit down with a list of positive and empowering claims, you begin to shift your mind and what you think which will shift how you speak and will shift what you see in your life.

PRACTICE:

Below are just an example of affirmations that positively influence, and impact me. Grab a piece of paper and write down twelve affirmations that you will speak life into, not just today, but *every day.*

I AM RESILIENT
I AM DISCIPLINED
I AM A TAKE ACTION KIND OF PERSON
I AM KIND I AM GRATEFUL I AM FULFILLED I AM
RADIANT AND FULL OF LIGHT I WALK
CONFIDENTLY AS A CHILD OF THE HIGHEST GOD
GOD HAS MY BACK I AM STRONG LEADER
 I GET CLOSER TO MY GOALS DAILY

I LOVE TO HELP OTHER PEOPLE AND MAKE THEM
FEEL IMPORTANT

AVOIDING INSTANT GRATIFICATION AND PROCRASTINATION

We are a generation of people who choose what feels good for right now; we choose to have instant gratification and it's been robbing our dreams. Choosing instant gratification has costly effects on our lives. It holds us back so much, yet we find ourselves choosing this instead of long-term benefit almost all the time Why do we do this? We are a society addicted to getting what feels good right now. We want what looks good right now. We want what tastes good right now. We want what sounds good right now.

But let me tell you this, the satisfaction of getting what you want right now is nothing compared to the payoff of getting what you want *most*. And the truth is a lot of the time, giving yourself what you want now will cost you what you ultimately want for your life. We are trading in our visions and deepest desires for our lives for a moment of satisfaction that quickly passes by. Every time you decide to skip the gym, you're giving up a part of your goal for what feels good at the moment.

When you decide to go eat out instead of cooking at home, you're giving up an opportunity to reach your savings goals. You're prolonging the process so much by constantly giving in to what you feel like doing or not doing in one moment. I don't believe we need to live dull lives by any means. I don't want to make it seem like we need to live a strict, no fun, no excitement, bland life to reach goals. I am saying that to have what most people don't have, you have to make tough decisions that most people *won't*. It doesn't mean you can't have fun, it just means you need to be more structured with your fun to keep what's most important to you, upfront. Having fun doesn't need to be throwing away all your progress for one night.

It's so important to enjoy yourself along the journey. You need to reward yourself. You need to have fun. You need to take breaks and enjoy yourself. You need to eat a piece of lava cake every once in a while. You just need to. Your heart needs these little fun occasions regularly. Don't dismiss that importance just because we're talking about avoiding instant gratification.

When striving for a goal, you have to be strategic with your decisions. It's a must. If you let your feelings always tell you what you should or shouldn't do, you will live a life of stagnation. Here are some ways you can choose delayed gratification instead of instant gratification

1. PLAN YOUR SPLURGE

We all need a splurge sometimes. It's when we splurge out of the blue that throws us off our game and creates stagnation in our progress. To keep yourself on track for hitting your goal and keep from pulling your hair out from lack of fun and relaxation, set designated times to do what you feel like doing. For me, that's when I get home from work for about an hour and then one hour before bed.

I just allow myself to relax, not work, watch an episode of my favorite show, and just do what makes *me* feel good. I'll also plan times to eat out like, Friday nights. I allow myself to just eat whatever sounds good. It's a reward for having been disciplined all week, but it's also a reminder to myself that I deserve to have a moment of bliss and just do, eat, watch, create, consume whatever my heart feels like. *Know* that you deserve moments like that too, but also know the importance of structure behind it. The structure will allow you those moments without breaking habits and making you feel guilty about caving.

You don't need to be on a strict system for yourself 24/7/365. That mentality is part of what causes us to break so often and give in to instant gratification. We get burnout and then have no self-control. Plan time for yourself to just do what feels good and allow yourself those moments in the appropriate time.

2. DELAYED GRATIFICATION

Choosing delayed gratification makes the result so much more satisfying. SO much more worth the wait. Saving extra for a car you want instead of the one you don't love just because you can buy it now. Delayed gratification is choosing to wait just a little longer for what you want most instead of settling for what you can *get* right now. You thank yourself every time you choose to wait it out a little longer to get something great instead of something mediocre. It's a hard decision and that's why most people *won't* do it. But think of where you could be if you chose the delayed gratification.

If you want quicker, faster results for your goals, you have to get good at choosing delayed gratification. Be very wary of the "shiny object syndrome", getting tripped up and distracted by a shiny new something and forgetting what you are working for long term. I have learned the hard way that living a life full of instant gratification is one sure way to prolong the accomplishments of my future and it is a great way to add stress and chaos in the process. I used to be horrible with this. When I turned eighteen, I booked a solo trip to Seattle. I had the hotel and plane tickets paid for, the only thing I had left to save for was food and any spending money on the trip. I had three months to save a sufficient amount of money for my trip but the whole time I would save money but spend it on things I thought I needed at the moment.

I was not keeping the experience of the trip in mind; I was thinking about what was going to make me feel good at that exact moment. So, the closer I got to my trip the more stressed out I was and the more I was running around trying to make up for what I had spent over the past three months instead of saving. Instead of going into this trip excited, relaxed, and secured, I found myself stressed and having to do a ton of extra work to make up the money. I ended up having enough to still go, but I ended up not being able to do some things that I would have been able to, had I delayed my gratification and saved as planned. That is just my very simple example of how instant gratification can rob us of experiences that are supposed to be abundant and turn them into experiences of stress and dread.

You know the feeling you get when you've waited what feels like a lifetime for something you wanted and you finally get it? That is a feeling we should ALWAYS be chasing. That feeling of pure satisfaction and pay-off because your patience, your hard work, your resilience and refusal to give in to instant gratification made the reward that much sweeter. It is worth it every single time.

TIMING IS EVERYTHING

There are two lenses from which we can view our lives. We can look at it from a perspective of "life is short" or "life is long". Neither one of these is inherently correct or incorrect, but there is significance in each way you choose to view your life. One of the most common phrases we use to motivate someone or get their butt in action is telling them that, "life is short." We do this because we want to inspire people (and ourselves) to get up and do what we want to do before our time on this earth is over. It's a completely valid motive because we should feel energized by knowing we don't have much time and it's running out by the second.

Knowing you don't have much time to do something you want to do, tends to be a good motivator for getting started. It lights a spark and gets us fired up. You feel a sense of "if not now, then when?". This way of thinking drives us to start up the dreams we've had tucked away for so long. This does such a good job inspiring us because we *know* it's true. We know we're aging, all of us are on our way to the end. We see it more and more as the years go by.

If that's not motivation to put fear aside and do the thing your soul has been screaming at you to do, I don't know what is. You have to decide what you're going to do with your one shot at this life. You will never be remembered for your fear, apprehensiveness, mediocrity, or by playing it safe. If you want to leave a legacy or an impact, if you want to do something great, meaningful and purposeful with your life, you have to take action right now because you aren't promised another ten years to do it later. If your life ended today and you looked at a reflection of the best version of yourself, who you were supposed to become, the person God created you to be, would they match? The value in viewing your life as "short" is that you feel a deep urge to do something, become something, achieve something, and to do it quickly.

The "life is short" lens creates urgency in our lives. With this perspective, we know that we are running out of time and if we don't act with urgency on our goals, one day we will look back and regret the things we didn't take action on sooner. We will wish we had gone for that opportunity we were too scared to. We will wish we hadn't cared so much about what people thought because it never mattered anyway. We will wish we had gotten healthy sooner. We will wish we had mended that relationship when we had the chance.

We will wish we helped more people, gone on more vacations, spent more time with family, reached more goals, tried more things. Life is short. So if you don't take action right now, there's a high possibility you'll never accomplish what you set out to or fulfill what God has assigned to you. We were all put here with a radical mission and a divine purpose. But only a few live to see the day their purpose and mission become fulfilled.

That is a shame. And it is due to many years wasted being upset about the past, staying in our comfort zones, or worrying about what people think. Its years of being held back by fear. I promise that at the end of the day, none of those factors will ever justify not going for it, working for it, and taking risks. Regret is not worth having a constant state of comfort and safety all your life. It's just not.

You have to understand that your time is limited and valuable and you shouldn't wait to start your dream. I've been tempted to wait a few years to write a book until I'm older and more "experienced" but that way of thinking is what produces the most regret for not going for our dreams. We always think that there will be a better time to start later. We always want to wait. We want to wait until we have our own house, until we have more money until we're older until we retire, until we get through school, until, until, until.

Until it's too late. And all we're doing is waiting to start our dream *until we feel safe*. We don't want to start until we feel the utmost security and when things are convenient. Start now. Start before you're ready.

There is no time to be wasted. There isn't time for you to wait until it's "safe" and convenient. You can't have regretted it at the end of your life. But then we can look at it from the other side of things. Life is long. We have been gifted with so many days and years and moments. I believe a lot of us look at life as too short, we feel like we've already run out of time or that we're too late in the game to start working for our ultimate vision. Maybe you think you've wasted too much time, but I want you to know: you are never too old to start something. But if you wait too long, you *won't* be able to start everything you dream of. Understand that if you're reading this, you haven't run out of time yet. You still have time. You still have chances.

What you do right now will determine if you live a life full of chances and adventure or a life of fear and unlived desires. So start. Start what you've always dreamed of doing. Start traveling the world. Start healing from past trauma. Start saving for a house. Start a business. Whatever it is, start doing the work and actually make it happen or you will always wonder what if. The great news is you have time, but it's up to you to use it wisely. You can always make more money, make new friends, get new jobs, live in new places, but you can't ever get your time back.

The chunk of time in front of you, however big that is, is all you've got. Please make the most of it. I know that no matter what, at the end of my life, I just want to be proud of the life I lived. I want to impact as many people as possible. I want to help and give and serve and create and try new things, travel new places, do everything my heart desires while I still can. And I don't know how much of it I have, so I'm hustling.

I'm making strategic plans for how I *will* live out God's purpose for me, for how I will help people, how I will reach my goals and be involved with my family. Life is short in the sense that it will pass you by and you aren't promised another ten years to bring your dreams to fruition. But life is long in the sense that if you do live to the average life expectancy age, you have lots of time and you shouldn't put off your dreams because you think you're too old. Don't allow yourself to be held back by the thought of having no time.

We talk ourselves out of so many things we could very well accomplish with things like, "I'm too old, I've wasted too much time, I've made too many mistakes". If you allow that to be your excuse, then that is where your dreams end. Use your time with care. Be diligent and use it well. Pursue the things that mean the most to you with full effort and intention. We aren't promised tomorrow. Almost every day there is a tragedy on the news, lives being lost by unexpected accidents and traumatic events. It's all around us and besides that, we will inevitably die. We just don't know when. It's never expected when we turn on the news and another life has been lost.

It's unexpected and sudden and devastating. I decided that when my time comes, I want to live a life-loving people well, pursuing my purpose intentionally, having the most fun, enjoying my life, and living gratefully and contently. It's not something that we enjoy thinking about, but now and then we need to tune into the reality that we don't have forever to do what we know deep down we are called to do. What legacy will you leave? How will you be remembered? We don't have forever, so it's time to get up and start working for the things you want to accomplish. It's time to forgive. It's time to let go. It's time to mend relationships. It's time to say I'm sorry. It's time to go for it, to decide what you want, to figure out the steps and to work at it every day What things do you constantly find yourself pulled towards? Is it traveling the world, swimming in the depths of the ocean, discovering beautiful hidden destinations, breathing in the air of new places, seeing what God has created, indulging in new cultures, collecting stamps on your passport? Start doing it today. Whatever it takes, if it's important to you, you will start making it happen because you may not get another ten years to decide to finally take action. Do it now. Start a travel savings fund, pick a destination you've always wanted to visit and work your way there. Put pictures of beaches and cities all over your walls, write it down every day, and make it happen while you have the chance. Is your dream to get healthier? Join a gym or start at-home workouts, go on walks, change your diet. Is your dream to start a business? Register your name and start working on getting the word out. Is your dream to have a life full of fun? Start doing things that are fun and scary to you, sign up for dance classes, hike a "14er", go on a month-long missions trip with your church, join clubs, life groups, and community. The common theme we are recognizing here is that no matter what it is you feel lead to pursue in life, it can be done only through *taking* action. And not just action when it all falls into place, not action when everything is perfectly set up and ready to go, I'm taking immediate action. There is always something you can do right now to get your goals in forwarding motion. Figure out what you can do right now and do it with urgency. I hate to be that person, but time truly is running out. Don't die with your dreams. Do, and accomplish as much as you possibly can in this life. Impact and serve as many people as you can on this earth.

YOU ARE NOT AN IMPOSTER

I didn't know what imposter syndrome was when I heard people talking about it. But I knew it was a clear explanation for how I'd been feeling about myself for years. I didn't call it imposter syndrome because I never knew there was a name for what I was experiencing, much less that it was a common struggle. Put simply, I was consumed with the comparison. With everything new I tried I immediately felt like I just wasn't good enough, and like a copy-cat. Growing up, I remember getting called a copy-cat anytime I did something similar to what was already done or being done by someone else.

I am all for originality and authenticity but I am not as innovative as I am creative. I bounce off of other people's work and turn it into my creative originality. I'm not the kind of person to just come up with a completely original idea on the spot. it's not realistic for every one of the seven billion people on earth to have a complete, original, never seen, or done before endeavor, idea, or creation.

I don't believe that was how it was supposed to be. As humans, we have been building off of each other's ideas and strengths for as long as we have been on this earth. That's the amazing part. We build off of each other. We all have a different cocktail of talent, charisma, strength, ideas, creativity, innovation, and vision within us. I believe that God intended for us to cultivate together, *not* to separate and each have our very own individual ideas and just pursue our ideas and never be like anyone else.

You are going to have things on your heart to pursue that have been done by someone else. The really hard thing is when what you want to do has already been done extremely well by someone else. Naturally, we sit back and think a couple of things:

1. I CAN'T DO THIS BECAUSE SOMEONE ELSE ALREADY HAS

2.EVENIF I DID DOTHIS, IT WOULD NEVER AMOUNT TO WHAT THEY HAVE ALREADY DONE

3. SOMEONE A LOT BETTER THAN ME HAS ALREADY DONE THIS, WHY SHOULD I TRY TO DO IT?

This way of thinking eats you alive. It's so toxic. It causes us to work out of a desire to stand out, and be different when we are on our mission for the glory of God and to move the world forward. The question we should be asking ourselves is not, "How can I be 100% original" but instead, "How can I use my gifts the very best I can with complete passion and intention?". You do not need to do what has never been done and innovate something completely brand new to consider yourself good enough or avoid feeling like an imposter. You *can* do what has already been done, but the cool thing is, you can do it even better because there are gifts you have within you that nobody else possesses.

Maybe our mission isn't necessarily originality, but greatness in what we are pursuing. Of course, what you want to do has already been done before. But what unique skills or gifts do you have to do it better? It's *not* wrong to build off of what other people have already done and made it better, in fact, that's what we *should* be doing. I love reaching goals. I love the feeling of reaching a goal and accomplishing something that was deep in my heart to accomplish. It was a lot easier for me to do when I was younger, I wanted to be a dancer so I got up and started training. I wanted to graduate high school by myself online so I did it.

I wanted to take a solo trip to Seattle, so I saved up and went. I wanted to start a business when I was seventeen, so I did it. I have always been the kind of person who if I made up my mind about doing something, one way or another, I made it happen. It was important to me and I cared about it. I admire that girl who sought out a vision and had enough courage to see it through. Part of me is still that girl but I'll be honest, me writing this book is the first goal I have gone after in a long time. For a while, I stopped achieving much of anything.

Part of it had to do with being a young adult and trying to figure out my life, part of it had to do with not knowing which passion I wanted to define me, and part of it had to do with imposter syndrome. I want to dive deep into imposter syndrome, but first, I want to talk about not knowing which passion you should follow. It's so stupid but sometimes I would lose sleep because I didn't know who I was or what even defined me. I like too many things. If I was on the Bachelor and they filmed my thirty-second introductory video who would I say I am? How would I define myself? If I had thirty seconds to tell you what I do and who I am I just don't think I could. I am an entrepreneur, photographer, videographer, a travel lover, an athlete, an author, a YouTuber, an aspiring real-estate investor, a network marketer.

I also design logos and play volleyball on the weekends. It's crazy. One thing I know is that you don't need to be defined by one passion; who you are is *deeper* than what you like to do. But I also know that the most successful people are successful in about one or two things. Not nine different things. The second thing that held me back a lot from reaching any goals for a few years was feeling like an imposter. I felt such unoriginality from what I wanted to do, that I felt wrong for wanting it.

I would think that because everyone else has already done it, I just simply couldn't. I would think about how many amazing travel photographers there are and how I shouldn't even try. I would think about how many people have already written highly successful personal development books and couldn't figure out what would make mine so special. I felt like everything I wanted to do was already so overly saturated or so highly popular, and to be honest, unoriginality makes me gag.

So I hopped from thing to thing hoping to find what made me unique and stand out from the masses. The flaw in this way of thinking is that everything has been done before.

We have to knock comparison. We are surrounded by people who have already done what we aspire to do, we tend to get easily discouraged. We fall into the trap of comparison and quit before we've even started. When you get exposed to people who have made it big with your dream, it becomes harder to think you could measure up. Understandably so. I feel inadequate and inferior to the people who are so successful in my craft.

I'm guilty of comparing myself to them a lot, thinking I could never do what they're doing and even if I ever did get to that level, something better has already been created. We have to stop comparing our beginnings to someone else's years and years of work and development. That is the biggest thing to stay away from when pursuing your craft. If you are looking at someone's success status after years of work, do so in a way that is inspiring and encouraging. If they can do it, so can you.

You have to start asking yourself, "What do they have that I don't". People aren't more successful than you because they're more talented, talent sure helps give a kick start, but when it comes down to it, success is reached through hard work. At the end of the day, it won't be about your talent. Talent gets you going but it will not sustain your progress and success. So if someone is ahead of you, it's simply because they got to work sooner than you did and applied more action. That's it.

Comparing your situation to someone else's success is not comparing apples to apples so there's no point in doing that. It doesn't help you. Look at other people's success as something to bounce off of and create your version of that success. Replace comparison with inspiration. Look to others who have achieved at higher levels than you as a source of inspiration, not comparison. If you do find yourself habitually comparing yourself with anyone, learn to replace comparison with inspiration or simply stop following them.

Comparison is so destructive to your goals. Comparison is also a choice. You can choose to be happy for people's success instead of comparing it to your own. I get such a cringy feeling when I see people close to me living out my dreams. I think it's a natural first reaction, but, as I said, it's destructive and in our personal development process, we must train our minds to react with excitement and enthusiasm for people when they're winning at life. I believe that getting our minds to react with excitement for people when they have good news or have reached success, is what is going to help us knock comparison. It's nothing but a bad habit derived from a feeling of not being good enough or inferior to others.

The good news is that, just like all other habits, it can be hacked and turned into a good habit. If you find yourself feeling inferior to those doing more than you, simply remind yourself of a few things. Remind yourself that you're on your journey and your time is coming. Remind yourself that just because someone else is ahead of you doesn't mean they're a better person than you, it just means they got to work sooner. Remind yourself of your potential and allow this feeling of comparison to instead be the driving force for you to get closer to achievement. Instead of comparing and allowing yourself to be consumed with a feeling of inferiority, learn to be excited about people's success and know that your time is coming. You even have permission to do it better when your time comes.

BOUNCING BACK

How you bounce back from setbacks says a lot about how your future will look. We all go through really hard things in our lives. Loss, tragedy, sadness, brokenness, darkness, pain, sickness, you name it: Jesus tells us Himself that in this world, we will have trouble. Life will get hard sometimes, it will get messy, we will get hurt- but He also says to take heart because he has overcome the world. (*New International Version*-John 16:33)

Jesus has already won our biggest battles. We have full permission to bounce back from whatever has happened and embrace the gift of our battles having already been won. We don't have to stay in the same fear, brokenness, pain, or shame. We don't have to stay in that place. Whatever is going on in your life right now that you don't like, you have control and you can either change the circumstance, or you can change yourself and how you portray yourself amid circumstances outside of your control. How efficiently do you bounce back from setbacks? How long do you allow yourself to be consumed by your setback? That matters a lot because although we should allow ourselves the time it takes to heal from what hurts us, also understand this, dwelling on what hurt you will never add any value to your life in the future.

You have to be willing to get up and push forward; sometimes before you're ready. Because we were called to move forward constantly. Sometimes you have to push forward with the knife still in your back, or heart. Sometimes you don't have time to fully heal and fully forgive to press on towards your goals. There is a time to heal and a time to rise up and keep going. I won't sit here and tell you what's right for you based on your situation. But I will tell you that if you're prolonging the process for any reason, you are only taking away time for what you can create for your future. Life sucks sometimes. Like it kicks our butts, no joke.

But dwelling on it won't make it better and it won't prevent it from happening again. Anytime I'm doing great in life like everything is just going peachy, I always remind myself that I will fall again. That's how life works. It's a constant flow of ups and downs. I know that when I'm on a high, I will experience a low again and I prepare myself mentally. And when I'm on a low, I remind myself that I will experience a high again. Here's the trick, the sooner and more efficiently we bounce back from whatever knocked us down, the sooner we can experience the high again.

The frustrating thing is that sometimes things we didn't choose or bring on will knock us down out of nowhere, but then it's up to us to get back up and brush the dirt off. I like to believe of it as character building. Get good at bouncing back because that is going to save you so much time. A lot of us, when we get knocked down, we stay there for a while because it didn't feel good and we're dwelling on it, or maybe waiting for someone else to help us up. Maybe you've been knocked down and you could stand up for a long time now, but your just not because you think you need someone to give you a hand. You always have God on your side, you have everything it takes to bounce back, to rise up, to keep going, to be resilient.

This is where your why comes into play. It's times like this when something has come along and knocked you off your path when you need to have a stronghold on your why. Your why will get you back up. Your purpose and your mission in life will propel you to bounce back because what you're working for is bigger than your setback. It becomes necessary to bounce back when your why is something beyond yourself. When you're on your "A-game" for a bigger purpose, you will always have a strong reason to get up and keep going.

If you find yourself having trouble bouncing back from setbacks, recheck your why. Why do you need to get back up? Who needs you? What are you ultimately working for? If it's important enough, you'll know you can't waste time, you'll have a reason to bounce back. When we *don't* have a reason, we *stay* defeated. When there is no big reason to get back up, try again, and risk getting knocked down again, we just won't try. Make sure what you're working for is valuable enough to take the risk. If it's not that important to you, that's okay, but find what is because success requires us to bounce back quickly. Have your moment, cry it out, get mad, heal, forgive, but get back up and keep going.

Have a sense of urgency when it comes to bouncing back because the sooner you do it, the more you can spend your time refining your skills and getting closer to your goal. Failure has a way of making us feel inferior when it's something we all go through. We all fail, especially when pursuing something worthy or great. The most successful people will all tell you that it's never something to be avoided, rather something to be embraced. Failure is not the end, refusing to bounce back is the end. With every failure, you have a huge opportunity to bounce back, to rise up, and begin again. It's when we refuse to take advantage of that major opportunity that we stay stuck where we fell.

Shame will have the last word in your life if you let it. It *will* make you think that you've made mistakes too great to get up and try again. It will make you feel like you're not worthy of another round, that you had your only shot and you failed. Don't let yourself get defeated so easily. Have some faith. Each time you choose to get up and keep fighting, keep working, keep going, you are getting stronger. You're proving little by little that the enemy does not have a hold of your life.

It's one thing to say it, it's an entirely another thing to get up and prove it. That's what bouncing back is. You will get knocked down, plans will fail, people will leave, tragedy will enter the picture. But the one thing you have that nobody can take away from you is your ability to get back up anyways and press on. When you stay knocked down, the enemy wins. When you rise up and continue moving forward despite the pain and struggle, you win. I don't care if you've not yet reached your goal when you get back up and keep going, you win.

End of story.

HOW TO PRACTICE BOUNCING BACK

1. HAVE A STRONG WHY AND REMEMBER IT WHEN YOU GET KNOCKED DOWN

As we previously talked about, your *why* is the driving force behind you doing *what* you do. It's the whole reason behind your work. Let's take this example – you get fired suddenly from your job, it's devastating and extremely inconvenient because now you're at a loss of income. Let's say your why behind having a job is to pay the bills and put food on the table. Although that probably is a very valid why, it's a very minimal, obligatory reason for having a job and ultimately, I know that kind of reasoning would not propel many people to urgently seek a new job. Now, let's say your why behind having a job is building savings so you can finally go on that dream vacation this year, or start investing so you can achieve financial freedom, or pay off all of your debt and become debt-free.

Those whys are *purpose*-filled. They aren't goals out of obligation like paying the bills, they are true dreams in your heart and you know how happy you'd be once you achieved those goals. Your why *should* excite you. It should get your butt back up and inaction, *fast-* *if* it doesn't do that, you need to find a stronger why.

2. BECOME THE KIND OF PERSON WHO ACCEPTS A CHALLENGE

I like to think of it this way; when I've been knocked down or when I've failed, it's like I've been challenged in some extraordinary way. I've been challenged to show whether or not I was serious about my goals, and whether or not I was serious about my intentions. Being knocked down is nothing more than an opportunity to show the world how serious you are. Are you going to accept the challenge or remain defeated? It's all up to you. I love a challenge. I love an opportunity to prove what I said in the beginning, to show how serious I am about where I'm headed.

You can't win this challenge if you don't bounce back. That's what it takes. When you've been defeated, take it as a challenge and prove yourself.

3. UNDERSTAND WHAT BOUNCING BACK MEANS TO YOU

This whole bouncing back thing will vary from person to person. For some, bouncing back means getting up and retrying the same thing with better knowledge than they previously had. For some, it means changing things entirely and pursuing a different thing for a season. For some, it even means taking a few steps back and re-analyzing their goals. Either way, these are all forms of moving forward and not staying stuck in the thing that sets you back. Understand what kind of bounce back you need in your situation- it doesn't always have to be some intense measure of action, sometimes you just need to take a moment to reassess the situation and proceed with a clear head.

Sometimes you do know exactly what needs to be changed and your bounce-back can be immediate and energetic. The point is, you need to do whatever is best for *you* and what is going to get you moving forward most efficiently- what matters is that you don't remain in the pit.

Give yourself the grace to restart the best way you see fit. Take the action you need to take to regain direction and continue moving forward.

4. DON'T OVERTHINK IT

Setbacks have a way of keeping us in a place of defeat. Whether it's shame, frustration, anger, fear, or brokenness something is making us
feel like we *can't* do it again. I know that when something knocks me off my game, it frustrates me a lot. It tempts me to give up, to stop trying, to quit. We can wallow in our inadequacies, our shortcomings, our slipups, or our misfortunes all we want; it's not hard to do that. But that's one heck of a way to create a miserable life for yourself. I don't know about you, but I don't want to be a miserable person living a miserable life. That's just not why I'm alive on this earth.

But that's what we're allowing to start to fester as long as we dwell on what knocked us down in the first place. I get frustrated and bitter when I think about the things that happened to me, things I didn't deserve that threw me off my game. It happens to everyone. Car problems, financial crisis, losing a job, being forced to start over, you name it. It makes us so frustrated and we could wallow in it for years if we allow ourselves to.

But if you want to rise up and accomplish big, meaningful things, you can't be the person who does that. You can't mope around and allow what happened to you *consume* you. That's what most people do and that's why most people aren't where they want to be in life. You have to stop overthinking about what happened to you, you have to ditch the "woe is me" mindset and boss up already. It's your life, stop overthinking it. If you want abundance and greatness bad enough, overthinking isn't an option.

You can look back ten years from now and remember all the things you allowed to make you bitter and miserable, or you can look back and remember what a great time you had making a significant impact on other people's lives despite the crap that happened in your own. Despite the inconvenient situation, you're in, despite the nasty things people did and said to you, despite whatever happened to you. You can decide that your life is worth more than to wallow in misery every time you got knocked down. You can create the story, you *can* decide what your memories will be. I highly respect the kind of people who keep positive attitudes regardless of what has happened or what is currently happening in their lives.

I understand there is tragedy that exists in our world and of course, there are things you can't just "bounce back" from. I'm not dismissing that factor at all, but there is a time to let it go and move forward with your life. I hate to see people allow what happened in the past taint the rest of their lives. Their lives become tainted with things that happened ten or twenty years ago. You have full permission to let that go. You deserve to move forward.

The people around you deserve to see you healed and fully moved on from the pain and heartache from the past. Stop letting the enemy have such a hold on you. To bounce back is to step out of the influence of the enemy and into the authority you've had from the beginning. I hope you can see why I'm urgently pressing you to bounce back and move forward. The enemy wants you to stay down, that's why he tempts us with lies like, "why even bother trying again?", or "You failed because you're not good enough" or "you'll be more comfortable if you just stay in this place and don't strive for more."

I am vigorous when it comes to the games the enemy plays with me, I put up a fight. I don't go down easy; sure I cry, I get upset, I get mad, but I am back up before you know it because I don't let the enemy have authority over me. I don't allow the enemy to influence my life. I get back up. Over and over and over. It is exhilarating and rewarding. I promise you hold that same authority in your very hands, you just have to use it. Practice using your authority to bounce back. Soon that will just become the kind of person you are; the kind of person who does not wear defeat on their sleeve, the kind of person who does not let the enemy win. Put up a fight and get back up.

LIVING IN THE FULLNESS OF WHAT GOD HAS FOR YOU

There is a correlation between God and personal development. I have noticed a stigma with the thought of having a relationship with Jesus while also perusing personal development. I believe that we become tempted to believe that whatever God has planned for us, He will be the one to make it happen. I think we feel wrong taking things into our own hands because we have been conditioned to put our trust and faith in Him. It's a balancing act because I believe having a strong faith in Jesus is important, but I also believe that doing the work and growing into your purpose is just as important. I believe one hundred percent what God says about me and I don't believe I need to prove myself worthy to him or win his approval ever.

I know who I am in Christ, that's not a question. We mustn't confuse personal development with a need to earn your identity in Christ. But I believe that investing in personal development allows us to become our best selves; the people God wants us to be. I have two core beliefs when it comes to Jesus and personal development:

a. **GOD LOVES US TOO MUCH TO LET US STAY WHERE WE ARE**
b. **THE BALL IS IN OUR COURT TO MAKE A MOVE IN THE RIGHT DIRECTION**

We have to, of course, do the work necessary to step into our purpose. God will always lead us and guide us, but we have to be willing to invest and that is why Jesus and personal development go hand in hand. I believe that a lot of people put so much faith and trust in God and believe He has a purpose for their lives, but sit back and wait for God to work miracles on our behalf without doing any diligent work.

And then there are those of us who take all matters into our own hands, leaving God completely out of our decisions in life. I don't believe that either of these options was how God intended relationships and living life. I believe that we pray for things if it aligned with our purpose, God doesn't drop it into your lap.

He provides us with the materials and *we* get to work. Too often, we pray for a cake and God gives us eggs, batter, a pan, an oven, icing, and a whisk, and we don't do anything with the materials he has provided. Submitting to God doesn't mean not doing any work. Whatever you pray for will require you to do work and develop personally. It has nothing to do with earning your way to God, it's about being the best person you can be and living in the fullness of what Jesus sacrificed *for* you. Personal development isn't taking matters into your own hands and leaving God out of the picture.

It's about finding the purpose He's given you, involving Him in the process of bringing it to fruition, allowing him to guide and lead you, but ultimately working hard on becoming the kind of person who can live out the dreams he's placed in your heart. God has big purposes for us and odds are, we aren't ready for it just like the Egyptian slaves weren't ready for the promised land. They had to do some developing and character building and skill building because where they came from and where they were headed were two very different places. So consider this your wilderness.

You've escaped Egypt, God rescued you, He has promised amazing things for your life, and it's on the way. But now you have to become the kind of person who can *handle* what God has promised you.

We have to do some developing before we can step into those large roles he has stored away for us. And that is our responsibility to become the best people we can be for the glory of God and the important mission He's given us. Waiting on God is an important thing. But solely waiting is not a good strategy. Wait on God and pray, but also work. Work on yourself and your faith. Work on building a strong character.
Work on becoming a strong leader, an advocate for the Kingdom.

Work on being more giving, healthier, more patient. Work on healing and setting boundaries and cutting out bad habits. Work on communicating better with people and work on the way you speak to yourself. Work on seeing yourself the way God sees you. Waiting on God is never just waiting. It's waiting and developing. I promise that working on these things won't interfere with what God has planned.

It's not disobedient to pursue better character or to work on yourself. Allow God to work within you and in your life, But also understand your roll in this. Follow His guidance, be decisive, make decisions, God will always re-direct you. But holding still all your life won't allow anything to come to fruition. You've got to take steps and develop yourself. God will guide your steps, but you've got to do the stepping. The *Bible* talks a lot about becoming more like Jesus. That is one of our most profound missions in this life.

We are to become as much like Jesus as possible. How do you think we do that? I believe we do it through reading the word, reading books, studying who Jesus is, praying, and meditating, practicing patience like He had, having a character of kindness and compassion as He did, learning how to lead people well as He did. Boom. That is personal development, my friend. That is why it's so important when it comes to the plans God has for you.

TAKE ACTION

So knowing more about the correlation between personal development and Christianity, How are we going to implement what we've learned? Take action. Taking action will look different for all of us. We fall into the trap of thinking that our lives aren't together and we aren't getting closer to our goals because not everything is perfect. We can't think that way. Don't strive for perfection, strive for serious progress in one-two areas for some time. My room is a disaster right now, I skipped the gym tonight to write, I had two chicken wings for dinner and three cookies. I could look at my life and see a mess. I could get down on myself for not eating healthy, or folding my clothes.

But I know my priority. Knowing your priorities and choosing accordingly is much more effective than trying to keep all the balls in the air at once. My priority is getting this book into the world. So my room will survive being a little messy for a temporary period. I won't lose the progress I made at the gym for choosing this investment right now.

There is power in choosing a few key priorities and letting everything else be for a little bit. I chose my book and I can take action on this goal every day. So, whatever your choice is to go all-in on, it's time to take massive action.

PRACTICE:

Start writing that goal down on a piece of paper daily, make time for it, eliminate distractions, make progress every single day. Nothing should stop you. God will guide your steps but you have to do the stepping. Your days should be filled with action and focus. You should be so focused on moving the needle. Don't get discouraged when it doesn't seem like you've made big jumps of progress, it's about the small steps forward that compound and takes you where you want to go. The regret you'll have for not going for it isn't worth staying comfortable right now.

So if you do feel regret, use that as fuel to propel you to spend the next ten years ten times better. Use that feeling as the driving force to do better so you don't have to feel that regret of inaction again. I got judged and criticized for my entrepreneurial mindset as an eighteen-nineteen-year-old. It did hold me back. It kept me from a lot of action because I was consumed with how people viewed and thought of me. Now, only a year or so later and those people have come and gone and I see that it was such a minuscule thing. I regret holding myself back because I was nineteen.

It did not matter at all what people thought about my business. At least I had the guts to start one. I should have followed through. I should have pressed on regardless of people's closed-minded opinions. I didn't do that and this regret is a nasty feeling. It sucks big time. If you've experienced inaction regret you know that it stings and it's enough to make you get up and get to work fast. It's an ugly feeling, you should avoid it. Five years from now, regardless of how old you are, you can either be ridiculously proud of the progress you've made and the things you've accomplished, or you can be incredibly regretful of the time you wasted and the ways you held yourself back. I held myself back a lot because I was afraid of what people thought of me or their opinions. I was also afraid of losing friends. I didn't want my friends to think badly of me, or not want to be friends with me anymore. Crap talk is one thing, but losing friends is something that scared me.

I was also afraid that my friends would spread rumors about my crazy business idea and taint the rest of my friendships. It made me not even want to share with anyone. But I can sit back now and say that I don't talk to most of the people I did a few years ago. Additionally, if any of my friends were low enough to treat me poorly because of a passion of mine, spread rumors, or talk down to me, then they aren't that great of friends anyways and that's the bottom line. You have to adopt that same way of thinking.

I'm sure your worried about what your friends or family will say, but sometimes when God gives us a vision, we're the only ones that see value in it. See it through. Whether people understand or not. Whether people validate it or not. Whether people support it or not. It's not about anyone else; it's about your life and the mission you've been assigned. People *will* talk. They will have an opinion, it's up to you to decide whether you'll listen or press on with your vision.

Any friends that squash your goals or spread rumors aren't that great of friends anyways. You need to keep going because they are watching. Either you will be right or they will. Your choice.

If nobody thinks your idea is crazy, it's probably not big enough. Have some faith in your vision. Accept the fact that other people won't see it for a long time, or maybe ever, but they will be right about you if you give up.

The beginning can be the hardest part because you have to push through so much disbelief, doubt, gossip, and opinions. You will always have to push through those things, but in the beginning, you have nothing to show for so it tends to be a lot tougher. Push through, prove the doubters wrong. I love it when people doubt me- I love it- it's fuel to my fire because people who doubt me don't know what I'm made of.

They don't know my determination. They don't know my commitment or seriousness; let people doubt you, and embrace it with a smile, and then turn around and prove them wrong. Try it, it's so fun. The antidote to fear is action. Sometimes we have to do it afraid. We have to be uncomfortable. We have to do it though we may be uncertain. We have to do it. Inaction will kill your dreams.

PROGRESS OVER PERFECTION:

There is a major flaw found within striving for perfection. It's much like people-pleasing; unattainable, unreliable, and unrealistic. Striving for progress? Now that changes the game. I get so much more encouragement and satisfaction when I look at my week, knowing full well I didn't do everything perfectly, but I did do better than the week before. Slow, steady progress wins over bursts of short term seemingly perfection. Because then each week you get to celebrate and have a party because you made progress.

Each week you're getting closer and better and stronger and smarter.

What's the fun in craving perfection anyways? What happens if you achieve perfection? What else is there to work for or accomplish?

We think we want perfection but we don't. Believe it or not, but we crave challenges, setbacks, lessons, victories, and new challenges. For me, striving for perfection has looked like purchasing a workout program from some random girl on Instagram, I go strong for about a week and then I miss a day or get sick or get lazy and I would start the whole eight-week challenge over. I dismissed my progress because I wasn't doing it perfectly. If I just kept going I would have been on the level I was working for by now.

Sometimes you just have to stay the course and not allow yourself to be tempted to start over because it wasn't perfect. If your first try at something is perfect, you've started way too late. Allow yourself to make mistakes and fail miserably. Just be better the next day or even the next hour. The other mistake we make is when we do have a setback, we wait a whole day or week or even a year sometimes, to restart.

You can always start over, but sometimes that's not what's best. Sometimes you just need to keep going and embrace the flawed process of getting to where you're headed. Anywhere worth going, anything worth having will take so much work and so much uncertainty. It will require so much faith and persistence. It will not require perfection, so get that out of your head. permit yourself to do it "badly" for a while. I had to give myself permission to just write and forget about all the typos for a while. Stop worrying about it making sense and just do the damn thing.

Being overanalytical kills our dreams. We learn best by doing so get out there and take action imperfectly. Your skills will sharpen, you will learn, you will get better, and stronger. But you *won't* if you *don't* start and allow imperfection to have its place in your life. Stop trying to fight it. Nothing in this book has been written from a pedestal of perfection. This is just my knowledge that I'm sharing with you. But applied knowledge with action is where the money's at. Choose an action that will give you the biggest leap forward and just go for it.

Don't allow yourself to become discouraged when there are parts of your life that aren't all put together. It's ok for things to be messy for some time while you focus on one important thing that has been tugging on your heart. Greatness of any kind takes a lot of focus and discipline. I promise that you will reach your goal so much faster if you make it your primary focus for a season in your life. And you will also remember how hard you worked and how much focus you had. You will be able to remember the experience so much better and with much greater detail because you weren't trying to juggle fifteen things at once.

For me, my thing was writing this book. After this book is finished, I want to focus hard on my photo and video skills; building my photography business and creating videos. But I know that right now, I have to focus on the task at hand and those things will have to wait for now. There *is* power in making that decision. I don't know what your one thing is. Maybe it's something we've talked about in this book, maybe there's something on your heart you've been feeling lead to pursue. Take some time to pray about it, ask God where He *wants* you and what he wants you doing in this season. I do believe it takes some soul searching to come up with the thing of most importance to dive in on, but once you know your mission, jump.

We live in a world of YouTube, online courses and webinars, blogs, and books. We live in a world of people who are on fire about giving their knowledge out into the world for free. I believe that we could all use a reminder that God has more for us. That our current situation isn't where we're supposed to stay. I *know* that you've been through painful things. But God is saying to you right now that He wants to restore the wasted years. You just have to open the door and put yourself in a position to be moved by God. Stop walking in resistance when
God is trying to take the weight off your shoulders.

THE FREEDOM YOU POSESS

You have the freedom to choose your thoughts, so, if I were you, I would make sure to choose good ones. In this book, we talked about the power you have over your thoughts. If you feel consumed by self-limiting beliefs, you need to exercise that power more. One of the easiest ways to do that is to practice affirmations. Saying a set of affirmations daily retrains your mind to think in a more empowering way. You have to change the way your unconscious mind operates because when limiting beliefs and self-doubt are habitual, your results in life will match it. It's all about exercising your power to choose powerful thoughts, as well as, reverse engineering your mind to think more positively, to think life-giving thoughts.

Where your mind goes, your body follows. When you can train your thoughts to be those of empowerment, positivity, intentionality, and confidence, you will be amazed at where you will be six months from now. Here is how I practice affirmations. I start by making a list of affirmations. I have three categories I want to hit on my list. First, how I think. I want to think powerful thoughts such as "I am a powerful woman", "I am smart", "I am confident", "I am strong", I am resilient", "I am persistent in pursuit of my dreams". This helps train my brain to think positive things about myself and my capabilities. Next, I list affirmations based on how I conduct myself. A few examples would be "I am enthusiastic in all my interactions", "I am a great friend, I attract great friends", "I am an exceptional leader", "I am kind, direct, and intentional in my conversations", I am a great communicator".

Last, I list affirmations based on how I make other people feel such as, "I make people feel important", "I am making a positive impact on people's lives", "I am the kind of person other people can always come to." Practicing these affirmations is the process of refining your belief system. When you are in the habit of believing negative things about yourself, you find yourself in the middle of ruts, not making any progress and not hitting any goals. You *can't* rise to the next level with the same negative thinking.

You can practice affirmations in many ways. You can write them down in a journal every morning, you can put them on a poster board and hang them in your room, you can read them out loud every day, or you can do all 3 and start training your mind to think the critical things it needs to for you to succeed. However you choose to practice affirmations, just make sure that this new information is getting regularly put in your face, in your thought process, and your words. I want to challenge you to spend the next ninety days retraining your mind with positive, empowering, life-giving affirmations.

I believe ninety days is the sweet spot we should aim for because if everyone is correct about it taking ninety days to create a new lifestyle, you will be ten times more confident, mindful, intentional, excited, impactful and influential in just three short months of consistent, diligent action.

1. YOU HAVE THE FREEDOM TO CONDUCT YOURSELF WITH CONFIDENCE

Another big topic we tackled in this book is how important it is to conquer compliance with assertive conduct.

People often get these two things mixed up; being rude and being assertive. Being assertive and direct does not make you rude. Being rude makes you rude. You can be the person who is direct in conversations, yet also be the kindest person in the world at the same time. You being assertive does *not* make you disrespectful, it makes you someone who has their mind made up and they aren't too scared to communicate that. It also doesn't mean that you can't be open to other ideas around you, it just means that you have the freedom to confidently express your thoughts and ideas.

When we don't state what we are thinking or what we want, we will more often be put in a place of compliance. We will have to go along with whatever the more assertive person wants as long as we continue to put our thoughts and wants on the backburner. As I mentioned before, I struggled heavily with being open about what I thought or wanted because I was playing small and trying not to bring annoyance to anyone. Nobody needs to live a life like that because people will get annoyed over everything, so you might as well be your authentic self in your communication and conduct. To be authentic means to be genuine.

How often are you practicing being genuine? I know people-pleasing makes it hard, but life is so much more enjoyable when we are living genuinely as our best selves. You can practice being genuine in your conduct by these three things that changed my life; smiling, making eye contact, and having enthusiasm. They teach this stuff in sales but it applies to one thing across the board; *relationships.* If you want better communications among your relationships if you want to present yourself more confidently if you want to demonstrate more boldness in your everyday life, practice these three things. Eye contact is important because it creates trust. Practice being aware of your eye contact in interactions with people.

If you can have and maintain eye contact with people, you will come across much more trustworthy and confident. Smiling is important because smiling makes you more joyful and it makes you look that way too. Joyful people naturally come across more confident because they are not afraid to share their joy with the strangers around them. Next time you have a choice between staying reserved, hiding your joy, playing small, or sharing your smile and joy, always choose the second option. Enthusiasm is important for the same reasons joy is, don't be afraid to show your excitement and zest in your day to day life. People are attracted to enthusiastic people. When you can master your conduct and start being fully genuine in your interactions, you will feel so much more at ease.

We are putting a massive strain on ourselves every time we *choose* to hold back our authenticity and act like someone who's not us just in an attempt to make people like us more.

2. YOU HAVE THE FREEDOM TO PICK AND CHOOSE WHO YOU LISTEN TO

Not all opinions are nonsense. But most of them are. A trap we fall into is thinking we *need* to accept everyone's opinions as truth and importance. The thing is, people *love* to have opinions about everything, but not everybody needs to have a say about you and what you do. We need to get good at weeding out irrelevant, pointless, random opinions of other people. To do this, start being extremely mindful of who is making and stating opinions. Assess and decide whether those opinions are important or not. To weed out opinions means to sort out which ones matter and which ones don't. There are plenty of opinions that won't matter in your life.

You mustn't hold onto them and accept them as truth because you will continue to overthink everything you do and you'll be back to striving for people's approval. There are some people (close people to me, in fact) who have had some absurd opinions about me and I just had to decide that I wasn't getting involved. Their opinions were so far off, I didn't even want to be involved in the drama it would cause me to try and explain myself and switch their opinions. It's not even worth it. I would just rather people have whatever opinions they want and I'll go manifest my greatness without listening to them.

This mindset changed my life because now I don't overthink nearly as much about what other people think or say about me. It is completely irrelevant to my life. It's relevant enough for me to understand that people will misunderstand me, mischaracterize me, and misjudge me. I understand that will happen and I expect it to. But it's irrelevant in the sense that whether people do those things or not, I know my mission and nobody's opinions are going to stop me. I've stopped allowing judgment from other people to make me lose focus because they don't matter.

I'm not wasting my time dwelling in the judgments people place on me and neither should you. You have more important things to worry about than what people think about you for trying. The person trying and taking action will always outdo the person sitting back and criticizing everybody else. There is nothing admirable about someone who just gossips and makes opinionated judgments about other people. So, don't sweat it. Practice your freedom to disregard opinions that don't matter; i.e., opinions that don't get you closer to your goal(s), opinions that don't help you improve as a person.

My rule of thumb is, and always will be, if the person making judgments about me or giving me opinionated advice does not have the lifestyle I want or has not accomplished what I'm working to accomplish, then their opinions don't get a place in my life. I want to encourage you to adopt this same way of thinking.

3.-YOU HAVE THE FREEDOM TO DO AWAY WITH YOUR PAST BAGGAGE

The issue so many people face in life is that they never fully move on from their past. We have all, in one form or another, had some past trauma, past pain, past hardship. It's one thing we all have in common. I think a key difference between the people who achieve at high levels and those who don't, is their ability to recover and overcome past hardship. The only thing living in the past does, is keep you there. You can either continue to live in the past, dwell on what's hurt or inconvenienced you, or you can move forward into bigger, better things.

But you can't do both. So many people think they can do both, but you can't. If you want fullness and fulfillment in your life, if you truly want to go to the next level of freedom and satisfaction, you can't keep carrying around what's affected you in the past.

I don't know what that looks like for everyone. Maybe that means getting help, seeing a therapist. Maybe it means breaking up with your toxic boyfriend, girlfriend, or ending a toxic friendship. Maybe it's confronting who hurt you, and maybe it's, once and for all, get over it. I'm sorry if that's too blunt but we need to hear that sometimes. I think a lot of people treat their painful pasts as a crutch.

I see a lot of people using their trauma as an excuse to keep indulging in toxic behavior. A lot of people don't want to give up their pain because that also means giving up their crutch. Then what excuse will they use when they want to do what's not right? It all goes back to what you want for your life and your future. So many of us want grand, exciting, new, amazing things for our future but we aren't even willing to let go of our past. How do we even expect that to work? Whatever you want for your future will take giving up your past. Figure out what the healing process looks like for you and get to it.

Be diligent and intentional with healing. Here are some examples: I want an amazing, strong, God-oriented relationship but I know I can't get that until I heal from the relationships that hurt me in the past; my wounds *will* carry over to the next relationship, jeopardizing my dream of a healthy one. Here's another one: I want an extremely secure financial life for myself and my future family. I want to make my own money, I want wealth, I want to be incredibly generous to those in need, I want to support myself and be able to give back. I didn't grow up with wealth, I did see my parents struggle a lot, they always had to work incredibly hard just to make ends meet, to feed their six kids and keep our home up and running. I didn't grow up learning a whole lot about money and I didn't come from a lot of money.

But if I carry that frustration with me everywhere I go, all I'm going to do is shove away every opportunity I get to create wealth. I have to let go of the past and move forward in the direction I want to go. Last example: In this book, you read a bit about my past and my childhood. I know there are so many of you reading this that have gone through similar things and even much worse. My past caused me to be angry and blame other people. One of my biggest goals for my life, which I'm sure is many of yours as well, is joy.

I want a joyful life. I want to love my life. I want to love where I live, who I'm with, what I do every day and everything in between. How in the world could I possibly attain that goal while dragging around the anger attached to things that happened in my childhood? Do you really think I could pursue a life of astounding joy and happiness and be incredibly angry about my past at the same time? The answer is no I could not.

You get the point. Everything you hold onto from your past will hold you back from your future. You have complete freedom and permission to heal and move on, and to stop being a victim of your past.

4.   YOU HAVE THE FREEDOM TO RESTART AT ANY POINT

Hitting the reset button can be so refreshing. We have the power to start over at any time- we can always create the life we want. Sometimes I think we forget how capable we are of hitting the reset button and crafting a fulfilling life from the bottom up. It might require some tough decisions, but it is possible at any moment to start over. It doesn't have to be some crazy uprooting of everything in your life, but making changes, getting rid of old, and inviting newness and freshness in will liven things up. It will allow you to build a solid foundation for the life you have in mind for yourself. It will also allow you to partner with God and do things His way this time.

Every time I have given it all to God, my life, my goals, my finances, my relationships, everything, I can't say everything worked out in my timing or fashion, but He never let me down. He showed up every time and worked on my behalf to create the life He *intended* for me. If things are stirring up within you to pursue, don't keep putting them on the backburner. If what you're doing in and with your life right now doesn't align with what you truly want to be doing, change things. You can't always flip your life upside down completely and start from scratch, but you can always do *something* to change directions and head in the one you're meant to.

When I feel like restarting, I like to deep clean my house, clean my car, clean my laundry, clean my everything. I like to maybe re-arrange my room and write out a new morning routine. I might get a new outfit or a new journal; whatever feels like a fresh start to me at the time. I like to make my surroundings new, my appearance a little new, and my mindset new. It is not much but it goes a long way in the sense of creating freshness. Sometimes all it takes are a few fun changes like those.

But it's important to know that we can make those changes at any time, and we should change things up regularly. We can't always restart completely but we can always make changes to bring freshness and newness into our lives.

5. YOU HAVE THE FREEDOM TO ENJOY YOUR LIFE

If there isn't joy flooding the premise of your daily life, you're doing it wrong. If you are a believer in Christ, you know that He died so that we could have life *abundantly* instead of life trapped and weighed down by sin and hardship (John 10:10.) One sure thing I have made my mind up about is that I will live in the fullness of all that the death of Jesus purchases for me. I don't do it perfectly, I have bad days more often than I like to admit. But I strive for joy. In everything I do, I aim to do so with joy in my heart.

I implore you to bring as much joy into your daily life as possible. Life shouldn't always be easy, but it should be joyful as much as humanly possible. Strive to soak up every naturally joy-filled moment as well as make it a point to bring the joy into situations of hardship. Some joy is natural and sometimes you have to create it yourself. You are 100% capable of creating joy, so do it as much as possible. Whenever your last day on earth comes, I truly hope that, if any-thing, you can say "I enjoyed my life."

6. YOU HAVE THE FREEDOM TO STAND UP FOR YOURSELF

I realized a pattern in my life when it came to confrontation or even just speaking out about anything I believed. It was like most people didn't want the Katy who stood up for herself or spoke up about anything or had confidence or boldness. They didn't like that version of me. They wanted the Katy who sits back, shuts up, and just goes with it. That realization came from times when I spoke up about problems at work when I spoke up about the way someone was treating me when I stood up for myself when someone's actions toward me were uncalled for. Naturally, I don't like confrontation because I don't like creating that tension when I'm not the Katy people want me to be. But I have learned that with each time I stand up for myself, each time I display confidence with my beliefs, each time I speak up, it strengthens my character.

I was not meant to be someone who sits back and never says anything. I was not meant to be a doormat for anyone. You shouldn't feel afraid to stand up for yourself or speak up about issues affecting you either; that's the bottom line. You have the right to speak out. It does build your character. It turns you into the kind of person who isn't a doormat for other people but instead someone who is secure in themselves and has standards. It is so important to stand up for yourself. Will people like it? Not always.

But it's not about what other people think of you for speaking up, it's about doing it because you matter and you're not a doormat. Of course, there are right and wrong ways to speak up, we went over this in the chapter about language and conduct. But if you decide to conduct yourself boldly and speak respectfully, there is absolutely nothing wrong with speaking up and out about your thoughts on something.

SEND OFF

LIVE IN FAITH

I was thinking of the perfect way to wrap up this book. I was trying to think of the best way to wrap up everything we just talked about and send you off with stronger faith, higher confidence, more boldness, and closeness with the Lord. If there is one thing, I want you to do now after all of this knowledge and information on how to improve your life as a people-pleaser: it's to live in faith. The amazing thing about God is that he meets us exactly where we are, we just have to have faith. I guess you could call this saving the best for last because even after all the personal development it's true faith in God that will bring you out of these pits.

You get such a sense of peace when you know God's got a plan for your life and no matter what anyone says, or thinks, or tries to make you feel, they can't take that away from you. It's a promise sealed in heaven. I see everywhere how much people want wealth. Probably for many reasons but a lot of people want their money and success and a big house and a fast car to do the talking. I think a big reason why people want a lot of success is to flaunt it in front of their haters and be able to say, "Look at me! Remember how bad you treated me? Well look at my money, look at my stuff, now I'm better." Me? I just want to flaunt my God and His faithfulness.

I want to say, "Look at what He did for me. You said hateful things but look how much God loved me. You doubted me but look how much God validated me. You pushed me down but look at how God raised me up. You scoffed at my ambition but look at what God did through me and my passions. Look what He gave me, look what He helped me achieve. He was on my side the whole time. Every time you doubted me, dismissed me, insulted me, criticized me, disrespected me, God was working behind the scenes on my victory." I am comfortable with letting God's work do the talking in my life. That's why amid opinions, doubt, criticism, and judgment, I can plant my feet firmly on the promises of God.

I can give it all to God, my life, my goals, my ambitions. I can trust Him because He is working right now on my victory regardless of what others are thinking or saying. God rewards faithfulness. James 1:12 says, "Happy are those who remain faithful under trials because when they succeed in passing such a test, they will receive as their reward the life which God has promised to those who love them". (*New International Version*) It says it right there.

Remain faithful in God and stand firm on His promises even when you're going through the trials of judgment and opinionated criticism and you will be rewarded with the abundant life God has for you. The word also says in John 16:33, "In this life, we will have trouble. But take heart, because Jesus has overcome the world."(*New International Version*) That tells me that although I will encounter difficult people, rude people, disrespectful, arrogant and hateful people, people who doubt me and question me, people who tell me that I can't or I shouldn't, I can keep my hope in God because His faithfulness is unwavering. Remain faithful in God and His promises and He absolutely will deliver.

He will work on your behalf to bring fruition to the dreams in your heart. He will replace the wasted years. He will restore the damaged emotions. He will take what was meant for evil and harm and defeat and turn it for good. That's why I can give it all to God. It was never on me to "prove" anything to anyone. God's faithfulness tells all.

No matter what, nobody can take away the promises of God, so I remain faithful in Him. Not my ability, not my talent, not my visions or my money – God. He rewards those who are faithful. My God is good like that. Do you remember the Crazy Cycle visual I created at the beginning of this book? Well here is another one, it's called the "Victory Cycle."

God puts dreams, goals and visions in our hearts to pursue.

God rewards the faithful and gives us victory. He fulfills His promises and blesses us for our faith.

We encounter difficult people, judgment, doubt, insults, criticism, trials and hardship.

We choose to stand firm on the promises of the Lord, and stay grounded in faith in Him.

This is how you get victory in your life. Keep your faith strong. You can't have the victory without the faith. God will follow through on His promises and you will be rewarded for keeping your faith, standing on God's promises, and putting your trust and confidence in Him. You understand that God will take all your hardships and pain and turn it into something amazing for your benefit, right? Do your part and God will do

His. The good news is God's an overachiever. You can always expect your reward to be better than you imagine.

Follow the victory cycle when you don't know how to handle it when people judge you. No matter what happens, no matter what people say about you, what people believe about you, no matter how your situation looks, you can always rely on the faithfulness of God. Your faith is something nobody can take away from you: that is yours and it is your strongest weapon. God's faithfulness will come through for you, believe that. If you are a believer of Christ and you believe that God is currently crafting up an incredible story through your life, then you are solid, my friend.

Nobody can ever take that away from you unless you give someone the power to do so. No, unfortunately, we will not have easy lives. That was never a part of the deal. But we can rest on the promise that God will be there through it all, He will supplement our strength, He will be our anchor when it feels as though life is sending us adrift. You can release your anxieties about other people's criticism and opinions. You can release that anxiety to Him and know with full certainty that He's up to something for your good.

Sometimes I enjoy when people doubt me or make assumptions about me because I know something they don't: I know that God is on my side and He will not allow my suffering to be wasted. Sometimes, when people make random assumptions about us, all there is to do is smile and know that God is up to something good. You may not see it now, *they* may not see it now, but faith is not about what we see. It's what we believe.

You *have* to *believe* that God is on your side. He loves you too much to let you stay where you are so I believe that in this life, you will often be challenged and pushed and stretched to greater limits. The process of refinement is not always pretty or comfortable but it beats staying in the same place, as the same person by a long shot. What I have learned is that there *is* a process of rising up. That process isn't always easy; it can be hard and messy and frustrating, but where you're headed is worth it Personal development is worth it.

The character building is worth it. The strengthening of your relationship with God and your faith is worth it. The becoming a more confident and resilient person is worth it. Step into that. Step into all that you were created to be, one step at a time with our God guiding you ever so profoundly. This life is yours, my friend, it is a gift, now rise up.

www.ingramcontent.com/pod-product-compliance
Lightning Source LLC
Chambersburg PA
CBHW031132090426
42738CB00008B/1054